BREAD BAKING COOKBOOKS

The Ultimate Guide to Make Your Own Bread at Home With 50 Healthy Recipes for Bread Baking, No-Knead Breads, and Enriched Breads, Snacks, Sweets, and Party Breads

Maria Clara

© Copyright 2020 Paolo All right reserved. By Maria Clara

The work contained herein has been produced with the intent to provide relevant knowledge and information on the topic on the topic described in the title for entertainment purposes only. While the author has gone to every extent to furnish up to date and true information; no claims can be made as to its accuracy or validity as the author has made no claims to be an expert on this topic.

Notwithstanding, the reader is asked to do their own research and consult any subject matter experts, they deem necessary to ensure the quality and accuracy of the material presented herein.

This statement is legally binding as deemed by the Committee of Publishers

Association and the American Bar Association for the territory of the United States. Other jurisdictions may apply their own legal statutes. Any reproduction, transmission, or copying of this material contained in this work without the express written consent of the copyright holder shall be deemed as a copyright violation as per the current legislation in force on the date of publishing and the subsequent time thereafter. All additional works derived from this material may be claimed by the holder of this copyright.

The data, depictions, events, descriptions, and all other information forthwith are considered to be true, fair, and accurate unless the work is expressly described as a work of fiction. Regardless of the nature of this work, the Publisher is exempt from any responsibility of actions taken by the reader in conjunction with this work. The Publisher acknowledges that the reader acts of their own accord and releases the author and Publisher of any responsibility for the observance of tips, advice, counsel, strategies, and techniques that may be offered in this volume.

TABLE OF CONTENTS

Introduction 1
Chapter 1: Breaking Bread.. 3
  History of Bread 3
  Cultural Significance of Bread 8
  Why Make You Should Make Bread 13

Chapter 2: The Fundamentals of Bread Baking......... 18
  Tools 18
  Terminology 22
  Tips 27
  Mixing the Dough 32
  Shaping Your Bread.. 34
  Baking Time 35

Chapter 3: Basic White Breads................................... 38
    Basic White... 39
    Sally Lunn Bread 41
    Cola Bread.. 43
    Beer Bread 44
    Beth's Potato Bread 45
    Simple French 47
    Honey French Bread 49
    Italian Bread 51

Chapter 4: Wheat, Whole Grain, and Multigrain 53
  Wheat... 55

    Basic Whole Wheat Bread................................. 57
    Basic Honey Whole Wheat Bread 59

  Quick and Sweet Wheat Bread 60
  Honey Wheat Cottage Cheese Bread 61
  Yogurt Whole Wheat Bread 63
  Brown Old-Fashioned Bread 65

Multigrain 67
  Basic Multigrain Bread 67
  Poppy Seed Bread 69
  Cornell Diet Bread 71
  Mexican Cornbread 73

Rye and Pumpernickel 75
  NYC Rye 75
  Salted Rye Bread 77
  Nutty Wheat Rye 79
  Mustard Rye 81
  Classic Pumpernickel 83
  Light Pumpernickel 85
  Dark Pumpernickel 86

Chapter 5: The Great Sourdough 88
What is Sourdough? 88
Sourdough Starter 91
  Making Sourdough Starter 92
  Storing Your Starter 95

Making Sour Dough 97
  Basic Sourdough 100
  Easy Wheat Sourdough 101
  French Sourdough 102
  Pumpernickel Sourdough 103

Maple & Walnut Sourdough 104

Chapter 6: Pizza and Flatbread 105
Pizza 105

    Classic Pizza Dough 107
    Dreamy, Easy Pizza Dough 108
    Whole Wheat Pizza Dough 110
    Chicago Deep Dish Dough 112
    Thin Crust Brioche Dough 114
    Spicy Corn Pizza Dough 116
    Thin Crusted Sourdough 118

Flatbread 120

    Pita 120
    Focaccia 122
    Naan 124
    Flour Tortilla 127
    Lavash 129
    Frybread 131
    Matzah 133

Chapter 7: Buns, Rolls, and Biscuits 135
Buns and Rolls.. 135

    Hamburger/ Hot Dog Buns 135
    Slow Buns 138
    Parker House Rolls 140
    Orange Rolls 142
    Lovely Tomato Rolls 144
    Rich Rolls 146
    Fridge Rolls 147

Biscuits 149
- Stir and Roll Biscuits 149
- Cheese Biscuits 152
- Angel Biscuits 154
- Baking Powder Biscuits 155
- Supreme Biscuits 156

Chapter 8: Snacks, Sweets, and Party Breads 157

Snacks 158
- Quick Pretzels 159
- Extra Rich Pretzels 161
- Homemade Crackers 164

Sweets 166
- Classic Doughnuts 166
- Delicious Sweet Bread 169
- Cinnamon Rolls 171

Party Bread 174
- Cream Cheese Bread Roll 174
- Casserole Dill Bread 176
- Whole Grain Cheese Herb Bread 178
- Italian Party Bread 180

Chapter 9: Flourless Bread 182

Loaves 183
- Gluten-Free Sandwich Bread 184
- Gluten-Free French Bread 186
- Gluten-Free Italian Bread 188

Rolls and Biscuits 190

    Gluten-Free Dinner Rolls 190
    Gluten-Free Biscuits 190

Fun Stuff 193

    Gluten-Free Pizza Crust 193
    Gluten-Free Soft Pretzels 195
    Gluten-Free Cinnamon Rolls 197

Chapter 10: Breakfast Bread 198

Bagels 198

    Basic Bagels 200
    Whole Wheat Bagels 202

English Muffins 204

    Basic English Muffins 204
    Honey Whole Wheat English Muffins 206

Chapter 11: Fruit and Nut Bread 208

Fruit Bread 208

    Banana Bread 209
    Brown Bread 211

Fruit and Nut Bread 212

    Cranberry Nut Bread 212
    California Walnut Applesauce Loaf 214
    Date and Nut Bread 216

Chapter 12: Present Your Bread 217

Shaping Your Bread 218

    Basic Loaf 218
    Coils... 219
    Bloomer 219
    Braid 220
    Mock Braid 220
    The Twist... 221
    The Mock Twist... 221

Serving Your Bread 221
Preserving Your Bread... 223

Conclusion 226

INTRODUCTION

Congratulations on purchasing *Bread Baking*. Thank you for investing in this book. Hopefully, it provides all the information that you need to start making bread.

The following chapters will detail the cultural and historical significance of breadmaking. They will also highlight important breadmaking techniques, terms, and tips that will help you get started on bread making without having to worry about whether you're doing it right. A wide range of bread types are available in this book, including white bread, whole grain bread, sourdough, pizza dough, cinnamon rolls, bagels, and more! Throughout this book, you'll find recipes that are the best of the best and will leave you and your loved ones feeling satisfied.

Bread Baking is the perfect primer for people who are just starting on their breadmaking journey, but it also has delicious recipes that experienced bread-makers alike will enjoy. With easy to follow instructions and vibrant pictures, this book will help you know what to expect when you try your hand at making bread. You will be challenged as you begin making your own loaves, but with these straightforward instructions, you'll never feel overwhelmed. Now is a great time to start making bread, so dive right in and make the best bread that you've ever tasted. Nothing compares to homemade bread!

Many books on this subject are on the market, so thank you for choosing this one! This information was carefully curated to be as useful as it can be. Please enjoy this book, and let it start you on the way to making some bread.

CHAPTER 1: BREAKING BREAD

History of Bread

Bread is one of the first foods that humans made, and even today, it's one of the foods that is eaten by most people across cultures. Some historians estimate that bread baking has been around for over 30,000 years, showing how integral it has been to the survival of the human species. Further, it has deep symbolism to humans because of its importance in human history. Without bread, how humans interact and behave could look incredibly different. We'd also be a lot hungrier.

Even before advancements in agriculture, people were experimenting with bread making. Since the early days of eating bread, breadmaking has become an art form, but for a long time, it was an innovation to eat better and increase the enjoyment of food.

We haven't always known how historic bread baking was, but recent research has found that prehistoric people would take grains and water and cook this mixture on stones as far back as 30,000+ years. We don't know the exact methods that early people used to make bread, but archeological sites have suggested that some of the earliest bread makers were hunter-gatherers in places such as Jordan. Archeologists have found lots of breadmaking history in Ancient Egypt. They have even found preserved pieces of the actual bread or its dough!

Early bread wasn't what we think of when we think of bread today. It was unleavened and very different from the fluffy bread that we know and love today, but it was this early tradition of breadmaking that evolved into the bread we see in stores and make in our own kitchens. Bread baking continues to evolve as we understand the science behind it more and come up with new technology. Let's take a moment to acknowledge how far bread baking has come, and then we can delve into some more of the long history of bread.

One of the most important innovations in bread baking was leavening, which allowed loaves of bread to become airier rather than flat. While in the Middle East, India, and Central America, there was initially bread such as pita, naan, and tortillas, eventually people discovered the transformative properties of yeast, which is what is usually used to make bread rise. Around 300 B.C., people in Egypt began to make bread using yeast. By using yeast, the bread was able to get bigger and fluffier. While flatbreads are good and still seen in most cultures, leavened bread became more normalized in civilizations.

Before 800 B.C., people had to use rocks to ground their grains to make bread. As a result, bread was full of whole grains and was heavier. Bread types like pumpernickel were commonplace in Europe and across the world until people began to create refined flour in Mesopotamia. They began to use mill processes that created flour that was more finely ground. As a result, this bread with finer grains became popular among the wealthy, and those who had this bread could gloat about the superiority of their bread (though this idea will later be challenged). From this time, humans refined bread increasingly to create the white bread that we know today. Not only are parts of the grain removed today, but the flour is bleached to make it even whiter.

Circa 450 B.C. Romans began using water mills, which allowed agricultural advancements, which, in turn, allowed more bread making. The Romans began the trend of white bread being deemed as the better-quality bread while grainier bread was left for the poor. We know now that whole grains have more nutrition, but, like in Mesopotamia, in Rome and other similar civilizations, white bread became a symbol of status, and breadmaking was an important cultural art form. Shaping it would become important to cultures as bread became more entrenched in cultures across the world.

In the middle ages, bread became an important part of survival. People started relying on bread for sustenance even more than they already had been, but in medieval times, bread also became increasingly culturally important and distinguished classes. It also was used as dishware! In Europe, pieces of stale bread would be used as a plate during meals. After the meals, the plate, called a trencher, could be given to the poor or animals or sometimes eaten by the person who used it. This practice fell out of vogue when wood was used for table settings in the 1400s. For some time, bread was used as the food itself and a way to serve the food. If you've ever had soup in a bread bowl, you can get a faint idea of what dining was like in the middle ages!

With time and industrialization, the making of bread shifted yet again. In 1834, the roller mill was invented in Switzerland. This mill meant that people could open the grain instead of breaking it completely. Thus, they could divide the grain more easily into its parts— endosperm, bran, and germ. This allowed better refinement, and bread during industrial times could be mass-produced. From then on, bread would be sold in full loaves, and people would have to cut the bread themselves. That is, until 1917, when people were able to cut bread mechanically.

You've probably heard the saying, "it's the best thing since sliced bread," and you've guessed it, sliced bread changed the way humans consume their bread. A jewelry seller, Otto Rohwedder, came up with the idea for a machine that could slice bread. His idea was met with some disdain. Numerous people doubted that people would be interested in such an invention; however, after just a few years of slicing bread, only ten percent of the bread in stores was *unsliced*. This ability to slice bread led us to the typical "American" bread, which is light, white, and cut just right.

In the 20th century, chemicals were added to bread to make it preserve more easily. People ate white bread increasingly, as it was cheap and had a longer shelf life than loaves of the past; however, as nutritional science became more prominent, people began to see that white bread was less nutritional. Because of the nutrients that are lost in the processing of white flour, people were becoming deficient in certain nutrients. Thus, enriched flour was created to add some of the missing nutrients, which reflects how packaged bread is sold today. Amidst all the changes in bread production, people still love to make bread in the comfort of their own homes.

The way bread was being made has changed over time, as has the way we look at bread, but techniques and styles are still passed down through generations with slight tweaks each time bread baking is passed down. Baking bread makes us feel connected to our ancestors, and it gives us the power to provide for our own nourishment. Plus, it is one of the foods that people love the most. While much of our bread is made in factories currently, there's something special about making bread at home. The history of bread is a long one, but it is full of joy, sustenance, and perseverance.

Cultural Significance of Bread

Bread is more than just a source of nutrients and a way for our species to survive; it is a crucial part of human culture. Imagine a world without bread. You'd go to a restaurant, and what would you have before your meal? There's plenty of appetizers, but in many restaurants, complimentary bread with meals is common. Imagine holidays without bread of any kind. Imagine never having a sandwich or toast. Forget the existence of pizza, cinnamon rolls, and tortillas. It's hard to imagine living without these foods because bread is one of the staples of human eating. All around the world, people enjoy various kinds of bread and are nourished by this bread.

Nearly all cultures have their special kinds of bread. If you think of a country, you may be able to identify bread that is important to that country. When you think of France, you think of baguettes. When you think of Italy, you may think of focaccia. Jamaica has a flatbread called bammy. India has a flatbread called naan, and Mexico has a flatbread that we know as tortillas. Americans have cornbread. The Irish have soda bread. No matter what country you posit, you're likely to end up with a certain bread. The lists of cultures and their bread could fill up several books! In many cases, the bread techniques have been passed down through generations and, accordingly, have important emotional significance to the people who eat them. Bread is not just food; it is a way of engaging with our cultures and the people around us.

Bread is good for the body and the soul. That much is evident in how we live. Through bread, people become more nourished and more connected. Breaking bread refers to not just tearing off a piece of bread for yourself but also to breaking that piece of bread off and giving it to others. Bread provides, therefore, both physical and emotional nourishment. People bond over meals and bread is a food that people across cultures can share and enjoy together. The word companion stems from the Latin words *com*, which means with and *panis*, which means bread. Thus, bread has long been correlated with togetherness, and it represents that interconnectivity.

Bread has great symbolism in our society. It symbolizes being provided for and being nourished. It also represents prosperity and survival. Looking at the idioms that use bread, you can see what this food represents. When we talk about something being "someone's bread and butter," we are talking about their livelihood. For so long, bread has allowed people to live that it is correlated with people's ability to earn money. To say "let's get that bread" means to earn money and provide for oneself and one's family, and "taking the bread from one's mouth" means depriving others of their livelihood. Further, "To cast your bread upon the waters" means to act with generosity while "eating the bread of idleness" means taking things that you have not earned. Bread represents more than just food but our ability to live in general.

Breaking bread also has religious connections. It's no wonder that many of the predominant faiths in the world emphasize bread as being somehow important. Even in ancient times, bread was part of religious behaviors. The Egyptians even had a bread goddess who they called Tenenet. Tenenet was not only the goddess of bread but also childbirth, linking the idea of bread to fertility and prosperity. Egyptians would also put bread on the altars of the dead, again showing the profound role of bread in religious practices even in ancient times. The spiritual significance of bread has continued into modern times.

Christians use bread to signify their faith in a wide range of ways, and it is one of their most important symbols. For example, Christians refer to bread eaten during the last supper as the body of Christ, their savior. Churches still eat unleavened pieces of bread to represent the sacrifice of Jesus when he was crucified and then rose from the dead. Further, bread is used extensively in Bible stores that teach Christians how they should live. In one parable, Jesus took bread he found among a large crowd and multiplied it to feed everyone, highlighting the Christian ideal of sharing what one has with others. Christianity is not the only religion that holds bread dear as a symbolic and ritual device.

Jews also use bread in their rituals. One bread that is important to Jewish people is Challah. They use Challah for various occasions and shape it in diverse ways to represent different ideas. It's used in various holidays and for the sabbath, often to represent the two loaves of manna that fell from heaven in Jewish teaching. Often, this bread is braided to represent arms that are intertwined, evoking ideas of love, and interconnectivity. During Yom Kippur, challah shaped like a ladder will be made to represent striving to reach for greater things. Each Jewish person can approach making their loaves a bit differently, but in all cases, this bread has deep religious symbolism and brings joy to people.

Muslims also view bread as a gift from God. It is used to represent all food and the nourishment of people. It is something that Muslims respect and they are not allowed to waste it because of how precious it is. Islam teaches Muslims to eat bread if it falls on the floor or give it to birds because it cannot be wasted. Bread also symbolizes eternal life to Muslims. The prophet Muhammad would eat bread as a way of showing how simple Islam should be.

Bread even has political significance. In the nineteenth century, problems arose in Britain when Corn Laws cause the prices of bread to spike, people became outraged at the bread prices and debated the pros and cons of free trade as well as those of protectionism, which could have kept the bread prices level. Bread started conversations among people to promote change and thought. Throughout history, an absence of bread has caused issues because of how many people rely on it.

You've heard the words "breaking bread," probably thousands of times, showing how the act of eating bread has come to represent the act of sharing a meal with other people. It's indisputable that bread is important to humanity, so get in touch with your ancestors by making your own bread and allowing that bread to be part of your relationships with others. Share your breadmaking with all the people who you love, and let that spirit drive your baking.

Why Make You Should Make Bread

Making bread is one of the most rewarding activities that you can do, and most people love eating this food, so you won't get many complaints if you start making bread for your loved ones. While most bread uses flour, even if you are intolerant to gluten, you can still enjoy bread through other recipes. The key is finding kinds of bread that fit your lifestyle and needs. Making bread provides enough challenge to keep you engaged, but it is easy enough that anyone can readily accomplish breadmaking. You are probably asking yourself, "But why should I make bread when I can just buy it from the store without all the hassle?" Well, the answer is in the cost, quality, and fun involved in making your own bread versus buying bread.

It's cost-effective to make your own bread. If you want to save some money, make your bread. For years, women (and some men) would start each week making the bread that they'd need. It may seem too time-consuming, but once you see how much money you can save, you may find that the time is worth the energy. A normal loaf of white bread based on statistics from the Bureau of Labor Statistics is $1.30 while a whole wheat loaf is $2.00, and elaborate bread can be as high as $4.00 per loaf. You can make two loaves of whole wheat bread for around $1.92, depending on the recipe, which means that the price of the bread is nearly cut in half. Comparable price differences can be found with other types of bread as well, making the price difference one of the biggest perks of homemade bread.

You get to control what's in your bread. Additives are often put into store-bought bread to give them a longer shelf life. These additives could be harmful to your health. While not all are bad for you, some of the long-term impacts of these additives are still unknown and understudied. Chemicals used to bleach the flour and keep the bread "fresh" have been connected by some studies to cause kidney issues and thyroid cancers in rats. While the effects haven't been studied extensively in humans, your health is not worth the risk. By simply adding more homemade bread to your diet, you can control how many additives that you are eating and know what's going into your body.

You probably can guess that one huge perk of making bread is that homemade bread tastes better! The bottom line is that store-bought bread can never taste like what you get at home. If you've never had homemade bread fresh from the oven, you're missing out. The bread you make at home has not been sitting around for days. You know exactly when it came out of the oven, and you can bake it exactly as you like it. Homemade bread is more substantive, and accordingly, it will taste more satisfying to you. You can find lots of tasty bread at stores, but it's hard to guarantee the freshness and the quality that you can guarantee at home.

When you make your own bread, you can pack in more nutrition. Many loaves of bread that you find at a store have been processed so much that they have less nutrition than homemade bread. Generally, homemade bread will have more fiber and protein, while store-bought bread has more starch. Store bread loaves will also leave your energy crashing more often, especially white bread loaves. Because store bread has less fiber and protein, it processed by your body more quickly; thus, the bread you get at the store doesn't make you satiated so you will be hungry again more quickly. Homemade bread, meanwhile, will keep your energy levels up and sustain you as you go about your day.

You get to customize your bread when you bake it yourself. You can't go to a store and choose what your bread will have in it beyond choosing the brand that best fits your wants. When you make bread, you choose the flavors that you want in your bread and the ingredients. As you get better at baking bread, you'll be able to make changes to recipes that reflect your needs and your wants. If you have special nutritional needs, you can be sure to reflect those needs in your diet. For example, if you can't tolerate gluten, you can make gluten-free bread, and with how expensive bread for special diets can be, you can save yourself the exorbitant cost. Similarly, if you're a vegan, you can have bread without having to scour the ingredients to see if it is safe for you to eat.

Bread making is a fun hobby. Maybe you're not a baker, but bread baking is so different from baking other foods such as a cake or cookies. To me, it is infinitely more enjoyable. Kneading dough and eating your homemade bread can be a great stress reliever. It can also be a way to bond with loved ones. Baking bread with your significant other or kids can give you some nice quality time together. You will be able to create memories and use your hands to make sustenance that will nourish your body and your relationships. Bread making can be creative and feel cathartic for many people. It gives you time to pause the chaos of your life and focus on creating something. You can use the time you use baking bread as a chance for personal enrichment and relaxation.

Humans have been baking bread for thousands of years, meaning that you can do it too without too much stress! Stop making excuses that bread baking is too hard because it's not that hard at all. All you have to do is learn the steps and practice them. After a couple of loaves, it won't feel so overwhelming, and you'll start to build upon your craft. Bread baking requires time, patience, and practice, but when you can invest those things, you'll find that the payout of baking bread for yourself is huge.

CHAPTER 2: THE FUNDAMENTALS OF BREAD BAKING

Before you get to the fun part of actually baking bread, there are some tools, terminology, and tips that you need to know to make your experience easier. This information will make your bread baking journey easier and ensure that you have the best odds of success. If you've dabbled in breadmaking before or have been around an experienced baker, you may have heard these terms and tips before, but it doesn't hurt to clarify. Most of the recipes in this book will limit the number of terms used, but if you look at other recipes, you might find more of these terms and tools being used. Any recipe can be made easier using the tips.

Tools

The tools that you need for baking bread are very minimal. Rocks, fire, and your hands would, in theory, be enough for you to create bread. Of course, modern conveniences make bread baking much easier, and with certain tools, you will be able to save time. You essentially only need a few mixing bowls, a cookie sheet, an oven, and your hands to make bread, but additional tools will allow you more freedom in your bread baking. Even a few extra tools aren't going to set you back that much money, so I urge you to invest just a little in this pursuit. Invest in what you can and forget about the rest!

Mixing Bowls

You're going to need bowls to mix the ingredients in. You're going to want a large bowl because many of these recipes contain a lot of flour, so make sure your bowls can hold eight or more cups (though, I'd recommend even larger than that). Most people have at least one bowl of this size, but if you don't, you should try to get one so that your baking experience isn't as messy. If you don't use the right equipment, you'll never want to bake bread again without a nice, large bowl! I prefer stainless steel bowls when I make bread, but glass and plastic will also work for bread baking. Fortunately, most bread isn't as finicky as other baked goods (like macarons, which can go wrong if you use the wrong bowl).

Tea Towels

Tea towels are important because you can use tea towels dampened with warm water to cover your bread as it rises. Choose flour sack tea towels when making bread because they are made of linen or cotton, which is good for covering the bread and doesn't leave fuzzies.

Mixer

While baking bread doesn't require a stand mixer, it will make your life a whole lot easier. With a stand mixer, you can use a special dough hook to make your bread. When you use this tool, you don't have to hand knead the dough, which can save you some energy. Stand mixers can be expensive, but if you love bread making (and baking in general), they can be one of the best investments for your kitchen.

Rolling pin

A rolling pin is helpful if you want to shape your bread into nicer shapes rather than just putting it into a loaf pan. While you can shape bread without the rolling pin, you'll get a neater shape if you press the dough out using a rolling pin before shaping it.

Bowl scraper

You can get this tool for as little as $0.59, so this device won't break the bank. Again, this tool is not necessary, but it can help you get your dough out of the bowl once it has risen. Using this tool, you can gain more leverage over the dough and not leave any of the dough left in the bowl. It's one of the simplest tools that will help you make bread.

Pans

Loaf pans are probably the most common pan that people use whole making bread, but there is a range of options you can choose from to make different shapes and sizes of bread. Invest in as few or as many as you'd like. While not ideal, even a regular old cookie sheet can do the job well enough. Though, for shaped loaves like baguettes, I like to use metal, perforated pans because they cook the bread well and are shaped so that the bread rises in an ideal manner in the oven. You can start with just a simple loaf pan and cookie sheet and then get more specific pans as you get better at baking bread and know that it's a hobby that you want to continue. If you want to make sourdough, you may also want to invest in a Dutch oven, which is commonly used for sourdough breadmaking.

Serrated knife

If you want to be able to cut your bread before you eat it properly, a serrated knife is a must. Other knives will not cut your bread with precision and make it a whole lot less presentable. Most people already have a bread knife in their kitchen, so this tool shouldn't be too hard to find. If you don't have one, there are plenty of inexpensive options that will do the job. It doesn't have to be fancy. You can also use this knife when rolling out the dough and shaping it (but even a butter knife will work on dough in a pinch).

Bread baking machines

Bread making machines are far from a necessity. I tend not to use them because I like the entire process of baking bread, but for those who want more of an automated process, these machines are perfect. They are incredibly convenient. You, fundamentally, just have to put your dough ingredients into the machine, and then, the machine will do the work for you over several hours. This is great for busy people, but it loses some of the satisfaction of making your bread the old-fashioned way (well, the old-fashioned way with modern conveniences). If you just want bread, these machines are wondrous, but if you want the full process, stick to other methods. I suggest everyone try the full breadmaking process at least once before investing in one of these machines.

Terminology

You won't have to recognize a lot of terminologies to go far in the world of bread baking, but knowing some of the behind the scenes of how bread making works will make you feel more self-assured when you start to make your bread, and some recipes you encounter may use these words.

Autolyze

Autolyzing is a technique you can use when baking bread. While this process is not required, it can make your dough less finicky, so it may be helpful for bread baking beginners especially. In this process, you stir the flour and water in your bowl, and without kneading it, mix so that no dry parts remain. After it is mixed, cover the mixture and wait from around twenty minutes to three hours. The dough will then be more stretchy and smoother. You can then add this mix with the other ingredients after autolyzing. This process may be especially helpful when baking certain kinds of bread like sourdough, which can be more delicate than other breads.

Knead

Kneading is a process used to make the bread the right texture for baking. When you knead, you create a chemical process in the bread and better incorporate the ingredients into the dough. Thus, the bread will be able to rise as the flour and water mix. This process generally takes around ten minutes to fifteen, and you can do it by hand or in a mixer.

Fermentation/Proofing

Fermentation and proofing refer to the time in which you let the bread rise after you have kneaded it. During this time, the yeast breaks down the sugar in the bread into carbon dioxide and alcohol (which evaporates when the bread is cooked). From there, the bread can rise. You may also see the word proofing used to describe proofing the yeast, which refers to a step in which you let the yeast and sugar sit in warm (around 105 to 115 degrees) water for around five minutes or until you start to see the yeast get foamy. Some recipes may not require you to add sugar while proofing the yeast, but you should do so unless told otherwise. Without proofing, the bread will not get the desired rise, so this is a vital step in the process.

Fold

After your bread has risen, you can fold it to release any air bubbles that may have been created. As you do this, you strengthen your dough and even out the chemical processes in the bread. You can accomplish this by taking the bread out of a bowl and folding it over several times, or you can even just push at the dough with your hands while it's still in the bowl.

Quick Bread

As the name would suggest, quick bread is a bread that takes less time to leaven. Further, you don't use yeast or eggs to leaven these breads and instead can use leavening agents, which include baking powder and baking soda. Quick breads include banana bread and soda bread. Many people like these loaves of bread because they are easier and less time consuming to make than other loaves of bread (though once you know how to make them, other kinds of bread aren't as hard as they seem).

Sourdough Starter

Sourdough starter is a fermented dough that people use to make sourdough bread. It helps encourage the fermentation process in the bread and provides flavor. There are several types of starter that you can use for your bread. You can buy some sourdough starter, or you can also make it at home. Sourdough, because of its use of the starter, is one of the harder breads to make, but once you learn how to do it, you'll feel less nervous and make wonderful loaves.

Unleavened

Unleavened refers to bread that has no leavening agent in it. Without the yeast, it will be a flatter bread and not have the same fluffiness as other bread. Most bread types that you encounter in this book will be leavened, but not all will be.

Yeast

Most bread uses yeast as the leavening agent. Some, like sourdough, will not. Yeast is a fungus that used fermentation to turn sugar into alcohol and carbon dioxide. The creation of gas creates a reaction that caused the bread to rise. Yeast is also used in alcoholic beverages such as beer, which will explain the beer-like smell you may get when making bread. The insignificant amounts of alcohol will be released during the cooking process.

There are varying types of yeast that are common in baking: active dry, fresh, and instant. Active dry yeast is commonly found in stores and comes in granules. You can store it in the freezer to extend its shelf life. Over time, it will lose its potency if not used quickly enough. This is the yeast that most of these recipes will call for. Similarly, instant yeast is also a ground yeast and can be used the same way that active dry yeast can. It will produce a slightly different flavor, but you can use this and active dry yeast interchangeably. Finally, the third main type of yeast that you will encounter is fresh yeast, otherwise known as cake yeast. Some recipes you may find will call for a cake of yeast. This is equal to around 2 1/2 teaspoons of yeast (which is the size of one single sized package of yeast). Generally, you will use that amount for up to four cups of flour. You can use up to six teaspoons of yeast if you are using more flour. The exact amount of yeast will vary by recipe, so these are only ballpark ranges.

Tips

Bread baking is something that anyone can do. Many recipes are so simple that older children could handle making them (with supervision). Teenagers could easily make bread autonomously. Even as easy as breadmaking is, some tips can increase your odds of success and give you better quality bread than you might have otherwise.

Be patient for the best results. Don't try to rush the process. Be ready to invest several hours of waiting. Four hours is an appropriate time frame for making most kinds of bread. You won't be actively working on the bread that whole time, though. Mostly, you will have to wait as the bread rest so that it can rise. As you wait, you can accomplish other tasks that you must accomplish. Allot more than four hours just in case the bread doesn't rise as quickly as you hope it will. If your bread is rising too quickly and you aren't ready to put it in the oven, you can retard the rise by putting your dough in the fridge. You can also make your dough the day before you want to bake it by allowing the entire rise process to happen in the fridge for several hours.

Don't stress too much when making bread. Many of the steps require you to make judgments, which can seem intimidating. It may seem scary at first, but most bread will turn out okay, even if you make little mistakes, such as not letting the bread rise long enough. These factors will impact the airiness or denseness of your bread and other factors, but it will still be edible. No matter what you do, you're likely to end up with bread if you follow the recipes, but it might be denser than it's meant to be, or the crust might not be quite right. The more you make bread, the more instinctually you'll be able to make judgments. Even just weather conditions can influence your loaf, so in many ways, bread baking requires some trial and error. This book will provide many tips to reduce the error, but every good bread baker has, at one time, made a bad loaf! Keep with it, and you'll see those tasty loaves are far more common.

Unless stated otherwise, always oil your pans before use. You can use whatever oil you'd like, including sprays. With grease, you'll be able to remove bread from the pan quickly after baking and transport them to a cooling rack (or you can even just put them on a tea towel or cutting board to cool).

Before putting most loaves in the oven, you can brush the tops with egg if you'd like. This will help the crust brown while still staying soft. If you want your loaves to be crisper, substitute the egg for some water on the top of the loaf. If you want somewhere in between, don't use either! Experiment with these options to see which you like the best for your bread, and for different types of loaves, you may have distinct preferences.

For normal bread loaves, you want to butter or oil the top after they've come out of the oven. By doing this, you will help keep the crust soft so that it doesn't harden too much. For fruit bread and quick bread like banana bread, this step is not necessary, but a little butter won't hurt the bread, so use your judgment on this one. If you don't want to eat as much oil, you can skip this step, but you may end up with a harder crust as the bread sits.

Don't be afraid to add more flour than the recipe calls for if the dough is too sticky. You want slight stickiness to touch when you're making dough, but not so much that you can't easily knead it. For many doughs, the flour is just an estimation. For normal bread, you should be able to determine if you should add more flour by tapping your bread dough with your finger. You should, for the most part, be able to tap your finger lightly to the dough without the dough sticking to your finger. Alternatively, you will know that you have enough flour when the dough forms into a neat ball and is not sticking to the sides of your mixing bowl.

Cutting the top of bread loaves can help your bread be lighter and expand without cracking, which is called scoring your bread. Cut a few diagonal cuts on the tops of your loaves. Do this around twenty minutes before you put the bread in the oven. A good tip is doing this when you go to preheat your oven. The slits don't have to be deep, just enough to give the loaf space to expand when it is baking.

Many people use flour when they knead bread, but instead, you can try using water. When you wet your hands, that will keep the dough from sticking, but at the same time, you won't have to add any flour to the dough. Added flour could make the dough denser than you'd want, so once you have the right consistency of dough, don't with the flour balance too much, or the texture of your bread will be off.

Artisan bread bakers often try to create steam in their ovens, so while doing so is not necessary, it can improve the quality of your bread. Making steam in your oven helps the chemical processes involved with breadmaking. As a result of this process, the loaves become taller, crisper, and have a chewier crust that's found in many artisan loaves of bread. There are a couple of ways that you can create steam in your oven. One straightforward way is to spray the sides of your oven with water, or you can also mist the bread itself. Avoid the lights of the oven as you do this. A second method you can use is putting water boiling water in a cast iron pan beneath your bread. Put the pan in the oven just before you put your loaves in.

You want to make sure that you preheat the oven a significant amount of time before you put your bread in. This helps the heat stabilize. Aim to preheat your oven at least twenty minutes before you put your bread in, but it doesn't hurt to preheat it even longer than that.

Don't quit if you have obstacles as you make your bread—the best thing you can do it practice and learn from experience. No matter how many tips I give you, you'll benefit the most from learning how to bake bread in your unique environment. The more you bake bread, the more natural it will feel to you, and the more fun you will have as you bake.

Mixing the Dough

Mixing the dough for your bread is the part of the breadmaking process that will probably take the most time. For most recipes, you will start by proofing the yeast in warm (but not hot) water and sugar. You will then add the other ingredients, except for the grains, which you will gradually add when all other ingredients have been mixed. Flour (or other grains) will go in last, and you will slowly add these to gauge how much you need to put in to establish the proper consistency of the dough.

The ingredients won't take much to mix, and for the most part, you won't have to do much to them before you add them. One task you should try to do is sift your flour. Sifted flour will get you closer to your needed measurement than un-sifted flour will.

When your ingredients are mixed, you will have to knead your bread. Kneading is a process that intimidates many people before they try it, and you can lessen your need for kneading by using an automatic mixer, but even when you don't have a mixer, kneading isn't nearly as hard as you may fear it is. It might make your arm a little sore, but the motions of kneading aren't complex.

Some steps you can take to make sure that kneading goes well is to find a large surface and flour it. Then, put your dough on the surface and start kneading it by pushing at it with the bottom part of your hands. Take the back of the dough and fold it towards your body then push it down. Rotate the dough in forty-five-degree increments and fold the dough towards you again, repeating this process until the dough becomes silky and elastic. As you knead, keep flour near you, so your dough doesn't stick on the surface you're working on, but attempt to utilize as little excess flour as you can.

The windowpane test is a fantastic way to test if you've kneaded your dough enough. You can take a tiny part of your dough and stretch it between your first two fingers and your thumbs. If you're able to do this without the dough breaking, you have kneaded it enough. In time, you won't need this method and will be able to tell that you've kneaded enough just by observing the dough.

Kneading is one of the most important steps in the breadmaking process. You should knead your dough vigorously for anywhere from five to ten minutes. Without kneading your dough, the bread isn't going to rise well as it should in an ideal setting, and the texture of your bread will be off. A bread that is kneaded well enough will become elastic and have a smooth appearance from being properly incorporated.

The mixing process for bread isn't that complicated, but it will require you to put in some arm work when you knead, but even then, you'll only have to endure up to ten minutes of kneading before you get your desired results. Kneading is very rhythmic, so one way to make it more enjoyable is to put on songs that you love and knead to those songs!

Shaping Your Bread

The shape of the bread is significant to certain types of bread, as well as certain cultures. You can shape your bread in whatever way you want, depending on your skills and how much time you have to make bread. As you make your bread, you'll find shaping styles that you love and be able to master those styles.

I'll go into more detail about specific shapes for bread later in this book, but there are some basic ideas that you should know before learning more about bread baking.

For the most part, you can choose whatever shape you want for your bread because shaping is one of the most creative processes in bread baking. Even pretty shapes don't have to be complex. The simplest shape is the classic loaf shape that you can accomplish simply by putting the bread in a loaf pan and letting it bake. You can also choose other styles, which you can put on a cookie sheet or pan made specifically for bread making, and these are the styles that often look fancier and will impress anyone you show off your bread to. Some require practice, but many of the shapes, even ones that look intricate, are easy to complete. A common shape that you'll see is a braid, but shaping can be a creative process that you can do; however, you want. It's one of my favorite parts of bread making, and each time I come up with a fresh style, I feel proud.

Baking Time

Baking is probably the easiest step in making bread. For most of it, you just have to sit back and relax and take in the glorious scent of bread baking in the oven. The hardest part is deciding what temperature to bake your bread at and how long, but if you use the recipes included in this book, you won't have to figure out this recipe as your own. As you grow as a bread baker, you'll be able to improvise to some degree and start to create your recipes based on recipes you've previously baked (which is a great feeling).

Baking times and temperatures will vary on the recipe you are using and the type of bread. It will also change based on how large or small you choose to make your loaves. A long, thin loaf will often take less time than a stout, dense loaf. Thus, monitor your bread as it cooks. Generally, you will cook bread from twenty-five to forty minutes. Denser bread may take around an hour even.

Bread in loaf pans will generally bake from around forty-five minutes to an hour. Meanwhile, flatbreads may only take around five to fifteen minutes. Thicker flatbreads will take up to twenty-five minutes. Round bread and bread baked on flat bakeware will take from thirty-five to fifty moments. Rolls and buns take from fifteen to twenty-five minutes. Sourdough often takes over an hour. Finally, quick breads can take from forty-five to seventy-five minutes. Bread is usually baked at lower oven temperatures of 350 or 375 degrees, but some loaves are cooked at higher temperatures such as 425 degrees, and sourdough often is cooked at up to 500 degrees.

You're probably wondering how you can tell when your bread is done, and there are a few methods that will help you know when you should take your bread from the oven. The first sense you can use is your sight. When the bread starts to become golden, it is nearly done or done. With this method, it can be hard to know for sure when the bread has reached peak goldenness, so you can also use touch to help you decide if the bread is done. Pull the bread out of your oven and tap on the top of the bread. If the bread is done, it will sound hollow in the middle. You can also use the cake testing method. You can insert a toothpick or a thin metal rod, and if it comes out clean without any gooey dough, then the bread is done. Like the rest of the process, the more you bake bread, the better you'll be at being able to tell whether it is done. Various bread types will also feel and look different when they are done, so keep that in mind.

The baking portion of bread baking isn't rocket science, but it does take attention, and you may be nervous at first when you are inexperienced at making bread, but you'll quickly get used to the process. The best way to make sure you don't burn your bread is to check in with it and track its progress. Ensure that it doesn't brown too much, and you should be good to go. It may be harder to tell how done whole-grain loaves of bread are just by sight, but using the other methods listed will help.

CHAPTER 3: BASIC WHITE BREADS

White bread is a newer kind of bread that was created when humans were able to separate the parts of the grain kernel. As been discussed, for a long time, into the twentieth century, white bread was considered the bread of those who were well-off. It was used as a status symbol in many cultures. More recently, white bread was fortified to have additional nutrients in it so that people who eat this kind of bread do not have nutrient deficiencies. Many people still prefer this kind of bread after years of indoctrination that it is the superior bread. There have been changes in how white bread is perceived, though. Today, it is the cheaper bread and is no longer just for the wealthy. White bread is incredibly inexpensive, especially when made at home. It's fluffier than other bread because it doesn't have the heaviness of the whole grains. White bread is an excellent addition to any meal, and it pairs well with most foods such as pasta, soups, and salads. There is a wide range of types of white bread, stemming from a variety of cultures and coming in a variety of shapes. There are a plethora of recipes that you can find in books and on the internet. I have compiled some of the best recipes out there to make your life easier.

Basic White

Your breadmaking isn't complete unless you know how to make a regular, old white loaf of bread, but don't worry. This bread, for its simplicity, will have a rich taste. You can use this for sandwiches, toast, and French toast! It's basically the bread you get in the store but better! This bread is more calorically dense, but once you taste it, you won't care!

Ingredients:

- 1 cup water
- .25 cup butter
- 1 teaspoon salt
- .25 cup nonfat dry milk

- 1 egg
- 2.5 teaspoons yeast
- 2 tablespoons sugar
- 3 cups flour

Instructions:

Start by proofing the yeast in sugar and water. Then, incorporate the sugar, butter, salt, and egg. Once those have been added, you can add the nonfat dry milk. Finish the mix by adding the flour. Proceed to knead the dough for several minutes. By the time you are done kneading, the dough should be stretchable. Wait for it to rise for about an hour before shaping. Put the dough into a greased pan. Let the dough rise in the loaf pan until it starts to puff above the top of the pan. With egg, brush the top of the bread. Bake this bread at 375 degrees for forty-five minutes.

Sally Lunn Bread

Sally Lunn bread is a bread that comes with a legend. It's said that Sally Lunn, an Englishwoman, went to Bath and sold this bread on the streets. It's got a rich flavor, and the egg adds something special to this recipe. It's no wonder that this bread is a popular recipe, and many European families have their own versions of this bread.

Ingredients:

- .25 cup milk
- 2 teaspoons yeast
- .25 cup sugar
- .5 cup water
- .5 teaspoon salt
- 3 eggs
- 3 cups flour
- 7 tablespoons butter

Instructions:

Proof your yeast in the water and sugar. Then, add your milk, butter, and eggs. Once those ingredients are added, mix in the salt. From there, you can begin to add the bread flour gradually. Mix until the flour is fully combined, and then knead for five to ten minutes. Let the dough double before shaping the loaves and then letting the bread double again. Bake this bread at 350 degrees for fifty minutes.

Cola Bread

This is a fun, simple bread that is distinct from most other breads in that you can choose to use whatever soda you want for this bread. You can use either diet or regular as well as colas with additional flavors added to them, such as cherry.

Ingredients:

- 2 tablespoons butter
- 1.125 cups cola of your choice
- 3 cups flour
- 2.5 teaspoons yeast

Instructions:

Proof your yeast in cola (preferably that is not chilled). Wait a few minutes before adding the butter. When the butter is added, you can add the flour a little bit at a time. Knead the combination for ten minutes. Wait an hour or so for it to rise. Knead it again before shaping it into loaves. Wait at least twenty minutes before putting it in the oven to bake at 350 degrees for twenty-five to thirty minutes or until it is hollow when you tap on it.

Beer Bread

Because beer uses yeast for its fermentation, it can be used to make bread. This bread is a loaf, but it has a taste similar to a biscuit. If you don't have any yeast, but you have a can of beer in the fridge, this is a bread you can easily make. With only three ingredients, bread doesn't get much simpler than this.

Ingredients:

- .33 cup sugar
- 3 cups flour
- 1 can beer

Instructions:

All you have to do is put all the ingredients into a large bowl, mix, and pour the mix into a greased pan. When it is in the pan, put it in the oven and bake it at 350 degrees for fifty-five minutes. This is one of the quickest loaves of bread you'll ever make, and it will still taste plenty good.

Beth's Potato Bread

My friend Beth adores this recipe, and she shared it with me several years ago. If you want a great potato bread, this one is an excellent choice, and it really hits the spot. I love the starchiness of this bread, and it is a good variation to basic white bread. This recipe makes around three loaves.

Ingredients:

- .25 cup shortening
- .25 cup warm water
- 1 cup hot potato water
- 1 large potato, cooked in water
- .25 cup sugar
- 1 cup warm water
- .33 cup instant dry milk powder
- 2.5 teaspoons yeast
- 2 teaspoons salt
- 7 cups flour

Instructions:

Add sugar, salt, and the shortening to your hot potato water until they dissolve. At this time, mash the potatoes in hot water. Add the two cups of water to the potato mixture. At the same time, add the yeast to the ½ cup of warm water to proof it. Add the two water mixtures together in a large bowl. When the mixtures are combined, gently put in the flour until the dough is the shape of a ball. Knead for around ten minutes. Let the bread rest until it rises to double its size. Shape it into three loaves, and let it double again. Once it has doubled, bake it at 375 degrees for about forty minutes.

Simple French

If you want French bread, this recipe makes it easy while still providing some of the highest quality French bread I've ever made. While this is my second favorite French bread recipe (next to the Honey French Bread), it's still one of my favorite bread of all time.

Ingredients:

- .5 cup warm water
- 2.5 teaspoons yeast
- 7.5 cups flour
- .5 teaspoon sugar
- 2 cups boiling water
- 2 tablespoons oil
- 2 tablespoons sugar
- 2 teaspoons salt

Instructions:

Begin by dissolving the yeast in the ½ cup of water and the ½ teaspoon of sugar. While the yeast proofs, combine the remaining ingredients. Let the hot mixture cool before adding the yeast mixture. When both mixtures have been combined, knead for a few minutes. Let the dough double, punch it down, and wait for fifteen minutes. After fifteen minutes, roll the dough and put it into greased cookware. Make slashes across the top of the loaves, and wait for them to double again. Brush the loaves with an egg and milk blend. Add sesame seeds if desired—Bake for twenty minutes at 400 degrees.

Honey French Bread

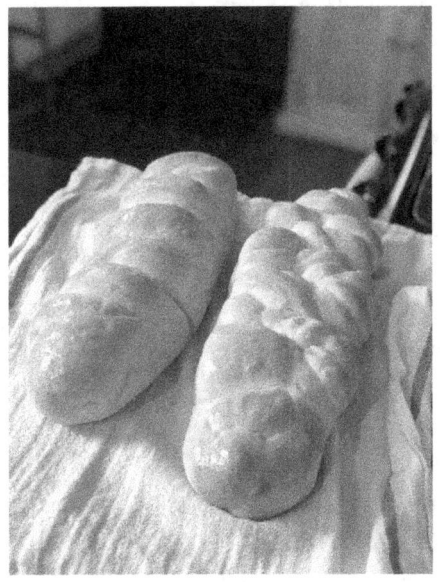

This bread is one of my favorites, and it's about as easy as bread gets. This is like the simple French, but with an extra little something. It's low fuss, but this bread always impresses dinner guests, so I can't rave enough about it. It's got just enough sweetness that it tastes great, and it comes out of the oven, smelling and looking just as wonderful. It is airy, has a golden crust, and it is great to shape into a nice braid or twist. I often double this recipe so that I can make three mid-sized loaves or two big ones.

Ingredients:

- 2.5 teaspoons yeast
- 1 teaspoon sugar
- 3 cups white flour
- 1 teaspoon salt
- 1 tablespoon olive oil
- 1 tablespoon honey
- 1.25 cups water

Instructions:

Begin by proofing the yeast in the water and sugar. After five minutes, the yeast should be ready to go, and you can add the olive oil and honey. I suggest adding the tablespoon of oil first and then using the same measuring spoon for the honey. When you do this, the olive oil remnants will make the honey slide right out of the spoon instead of sticking. Add the salt next. Then, slowly add the flour cup by cup. Knead the dough for around ten minutes. Cover it with a cloth dampened by warm water, and place it in a balmy location to rise. After one hour or so, the dough should have doubled. From there, you can shape the dough and put on greased pans. Let it rise for another thirty minutes as the oven preheats. Bake this bread at 400 degrees for twenty to twenty-five minutes, and be sure to brush it with butter when it comes out. Wait for it to cool for easier cutting, but it tastes so good warm!

Italian Bread

The Italians are known for their delicious bread, and you can get a taste of it in your own home. With only five ingredients, this bread couldn't get any easier. It gets a nice crisp crust, and it will be light in your mouth. This is another favorite of mine, and whenever it's one of my highly requested loaves of bread. This is another one that people may love so much that you'll have to double it when you're having dinner parties or hosting family events.

Ingredients:

- 1.33 cups water
- 2.5 teaspoons sugar
- 2.5 teaspoons yeast
- 3 cups flour
- 1.25 teaspoons salt

Instructions:

In a big bowl, proof your yeast in the water and sugar mix for five minutes. When it is proofed, add the sugar. When the sugar is incorporated, add the flour. Add the flour one cup at a time Mix thoroughly and then knead the dough until it is an adequate texture— stretchy and smooth. Allow your bread to rise in a warm area for about forty-five minutes. It should become double in size. Knead it again, and shape it into loaves before letting it rest for another forty-five minutes. Preheat the oven for 400 degrees as it rests, and bake it for around twenty minutes.

CHAPTER 4: WHEAT, WHOLE GRAIN, AND MULTIGRAIN

Wheat, whole grain, and multigrain breads are often denser than white breads, and they tend to be more satiating because of this. Further, they are packed full of nutrients due to the limited processing process that their ingredients have gone through. While these recipes may not be what you are used to, you may find that the more you have them, the more you love these delicious breads. Whether you're trying to lead a healthier lifestyle or you just want to experiment with new flavors, these breads will leave you satisfied and will challenge your breadmaking skills a bit more than the basic white loaves of bread. Fear not, these recipes are still fairly easy, and they will be a breeze once you have actually made them because the learning curve is marginal. If you're looking to improve your health by making bread at home, these breads are great options for you and have a wide range of flavors.

To understand these breads, you have to understand what whole grains are. Breads in this chapter will contain grains that have all three parts of the kernel, the endosperm, bran, and the germ. In white breads, only the endosperm is used in the flour, leaving out important nutrients. As you can see in the illustration of a grain kernel, there's much nutritional value found in the parts of the grain that are removed to make white flour. The most nutritious parts, the bran, and germ are eliminated in processing. Thus, by making grainy bread, you can improve your nutrition and feel better about what you are putting in your body. Whole grains are especially good for those with conditions such as diabetes, heart conditions, and high blood pressure, but anyone can benefit from them. With that being said, some of these breads may contain more whole grains than others.

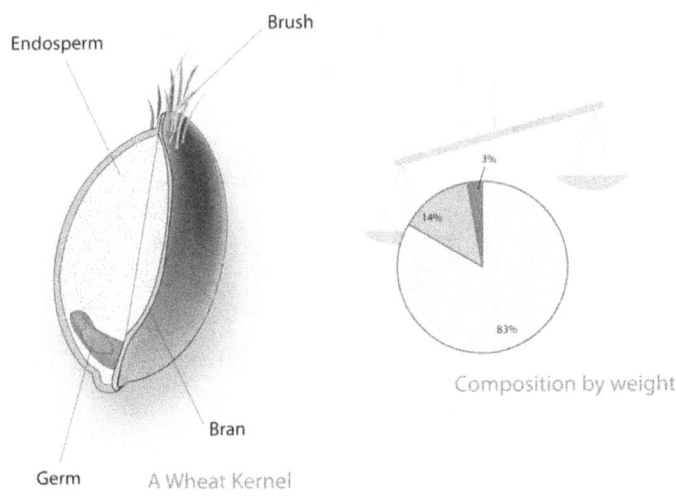

A Wheat Kernel

Composition by weight

	Carb./g	Protein/g	Fat/g	Fiber/g	Iron (% daily req.)	Others
Bran	63	16	3	43	59	vitamin Bs
Endosperm	79	7	0	4	7	
Germ	52	23	10	14	35	vitamin Bs omega-3/6 lipids

Nutritional Value (per 100g)

Wheat

Wheat bread is a type of whole-grain bread, but it does not have to have a 100% whole grains in it. Thus, these will be the less dense whole-grain bread found in this book. Wheat breads with some white flour in them can be an effective way to get used to more grainy breads into your diet without sacrificing the fluffiness of white bread completely. They will taste and feel more like white breads while still having increased nutritional benefits. They're also simple to make and require few additional ingredients to what you probably already have in your kitchen.

Basic Whole Wheat Bread

This basic whole wheat bread is nothing fancy, but it will hit the spot and be an ideal everyday bread. Feel free to double this recipe if you'd like to make multiple large loaves at once, but this bread should make a significant amount of dough, and all the flour it contains might be too much for stand mixers if you do double it, so keep that in mind.

Ingredients:

- .5 cup milk
- 4.5 teaspoons dry yeast
- 2 teaspoons salt
- .5 cup wheat germ
- 1.5 cups water
- 2 tablespoons sugar
- 2 tablespoons oil (of choice)
- 6 cups of flour

Instructions:

To begin, proof the yeast in the sugar and warm water. Once the yeast is proofed, mix the milk and oil in with the yeast mixture. Add the salt and wheat germ and mix until they are incorporated. Add the flour until you get a good dough texture that you can work with. Take the dough out and knead it. Gradually incorporate the flour until the dough is not as sticky while still being a spongey texture. Let the dough rise for around an hour or until it has double. Put your dough in a greased loaf pan, and you should wait for the dough to double again. Preheat the oven to 400 degrees. Pierce your loaves using fork tongues to release air bubbles and place in the over. When you place the loaves in the oven, turn the temperature down to 350 right away. Then, bake the bread for twenty-five to thirty minutes. You'll know that it's done when it is golden on top.

Basic Honey Whole Wheat Bread

This is another easy whole wheat bread that will leave you wanting more. It is easy to slice, and it is a bread-making staple. This recipe can be easily doubled to make two large loaves for those of you who have a lot of mouths to feed or just really love bread! You can't go wrong with this bread.

Ingredients:

- 4 cups whole wheat flour
- .5 cup honey
- 3 tablespoons vital gluten (optional)
- .5 teaspoon salt
- 1.5 cup water or milk
- 2.5 teaspoons yeast

Instructions:

Proof yeast in honey and water/milk (make sure it's not cold). Add the rest of the ingredients once the yeast is proofed, saving the grains for the end. Add your flour and vital gluten (if you're using it). Knead the dough until it is stretchable. Wait for it to double. Once it has doubled, shape it, put it in a greased loaf pan. Once it is in the pan, allow it to sit for an additional half an hour or until it has risen over the lip of the pan just a bit. In a 350 degree oven, bake for around twenty-five to thirty minutes.

Quick and Sweet Wheat Bread

This recipe won't take you long to make, and you'll be delighted by the sweetness of this whole wheat bread. It does not use yeast, so you do not need to wait for it to rise. It will more resemble a fruit bread than a traditional loaf, but it is still considered a wheat bread.

Ingredients:

- 1 teaspoon baking soda
- .25 teaspoon salt
- 1 teaspoon orange or lemon peel
- 2.5 cup whole wheat flour
- .5 teaspoon cinnamon

Instructions:

Begin by sifting the dry ingredients. Once you have thoroughly sifted the dry ingredients, add the beaten egg, shortening, brown sugar, molasses, and lemon or orange peel. You will alternate between adding the dry ingredients and the yogurt to the egg mixture. Mix until all ingredients are combined. At this time, you can add dates, raisins, or nuts if you please. This recipe should be baked at one hour at 350 degrees. It does not need tome to rise.

Honey Wheat Cottage Cheese Bread

The cottage cheese in this bread gives it an excellent, moist texture. This bread tastes fancier while still being simple to make. You'll impress your friends with this one! The egg also adds a richness to this bread, and it gives it a yellow hue.

Ingredients:

- 2 cups whole wheat flour
- .5 cup honey
- 2 tablespoons sugar
- 1.5 cups water
- 1 egg
- 5 teaspoons yeast
- 1 cup cottage cheese
- 3 teaspoons salt
- 4.5 cups white flour

Instructions:

Begin by heating the water, honey, cottage cheese, and butter until they are warm (but not too hot). Then, add the salt, yeast, and sugar. Temper the egg so that it doesn't cook when adding it to the mixture. In a bigger dish, add the warm mixture to the whole wheat flour. Once the two cups of flour are mixed, slowly add any flour that remains. Let the dough rise to double its size, punch it down, and then split it into loaves. Bake around thirty minutes until the bread is golden, and you can tap it, and it sounds hollow. When it comes out of the oven, brush the bread with honey and butter while the bread is still warm.

Yogurt Whole Wheat Bread

This is a whole wheat bread but with a twist. It may seem strange to put yogurt in bread, but fear not, the yogurt gives this bread an extra something that gives a boost of flavor and keeps this bread moist. This bread also has oats included, which add an extra grain and give it a great texture.

Ingredients:

- 1.33 cups yogurt (plain, nonfat)
- 2 cups white flour
- 2 teaspoons salt
- 2.5 teaspoons yeast
- 1.33 cups whole wheat flour
- .66 cups oats
- 3 tablespoons sugar
- 3 tablespoons butter
- 5 tablespoons water

Instructions:

Proof the yeast in the water and sugar. Then, add the yogurt and butter to the yeast mix. Add the salt. Then add oats and wheat flour. Finish by adding the bread flour slowly until you get the right texture. Knead the dough, let it rest for around an hour. When it has rested, knead it again before putting it into a greased loaf pan.

Let it rise so that the dough rises just over the top of the pan. In a 375 degree oven, bake for approximately thirty-five minutes.

Brown Old-Fashioned Bread

The brown, old fashioned bread is a tasty bread that's a little bit more elaborate than your basic wheat bread, but it's still simple to make and won't take too long. This bread does well being frozen, so you can pop it into the freezer if you don't want to use it right away and then bring it out when you need it.

Ingredients:

- .75 cups molasses
- 3 cups white flour
- .75 cups warm water
- 1 cup sugar
- 1 medium-sized potato
- 3 tablespoons shortening or oil
- 5 cups whole wheat flour
- 5 teaspoons dry yeast
- 2 cups scalded milk
- 2 teaspoons salt

Instructions:

Begin by cooking your potato, and then you should mash it. Combine the shortening, salt, and the potato as you begin to proof the yeast in the water and the sugar. Mix the molasses and milk with the potato mixture. Put in the yeast mixture. Then, incorporate both flours. Let the dough rise for around half an hour or until it looks puffy. When it has risen, punch the dough down and let it rise before shaping and putting into pans. Let it rise once more. Then, you can bake your loaves at 375 degrees from forty-five to fifty minutes.

Multigrain

Multigrain is another type of whole grain braid. As the name implies, this bread will have multiple grains. These breads generally have more ingredients than other breads, and you might not have these ingredients handy in your kitchen, so they will require extra preparation, but they are fantastic breads that will have great flavor and fill you up. Multigrain breads are super nutritious and satisfying because they give you a variety of grains, which have diverse nutrients. These breads can include any number of grains, including seeds, buckwheat, oatmeal, rye, cornmeal, and flour.

Basic Multigrain Bread

For a simple multigrain bread, this recipe is ideal. This bread will be full of richness and have plenty of nutrients in it for those of you who are health conscious.

Ingredients:

- 1.33 tablespoons fruit juice concentrate
- 2 teaspoons yeast
- 2 tablespoons honey
- 1 teaspoons salt
- .66 cup rye flour
- 3 tablespoons vital gluten (optional)

- 1.33 cups water
- .66 cup oats
- 2.66 cups whole wheat flour

Instructions:

Proof the yeast for five minutes in water/milk and the honey. Add the fruit concentrate to the yeast mix. Then, add the salt and vital gluten. Once those are added, you can begin adding your grains— oats, rye flour, and whole wheat flour. Knead your dough for ten minutes before letting it rest for an hour. Knead again after punching it down in the bowl. Then, form your bread into a loaf shape, and place on your greased pan. Let it sit for another forty-five minutes or until it has sufficiently risen—Bake at 450 degrees for forty-five minutes to one hour.

Poppy Seed Bread

This is another quick bread that will resemble fruit bread and have some extra sweetness. It combines poppy seeds and flour to great a healthy, whole grain bread that will hit the spot and can be sweetened with a glaze.

Ingredients:

- 1.5 cups milk
- 1.125 cups oil
- 1 teaspoon almond extract
- 1.5 teaspoons baking powder
- 1 tablespoon vanilla extract
- .33 cup poppy seeds
- 2 ½ cups sugar
- 3 cups flour
- 3 eggs

Glaze:

- .5 teaspoon of almond extract
- .5 teaspoon of milk
- .33 cups powdered sugar
- 3 teaspoons of softened butter

Instructions:

Combine all ingredients in the order listed and mix them by hand or in a mixer. Pour the mix into ungreased pans. When your dough has been divided, bake the loaves at 350 degrees for about one hour. To ensure that your bread is done, you can use the toothpick method to see that it is done. Like all quick bread, you'll want to wait before removing this bread from the pan so that it has time to cool a bit like you would with a cake. Put the glaze on while still warm, and feel free to sprinkle on some sliced almonds.

Glaze:

Combine all the ingredients and pour them over the bread while it is warm.

Cornell Diet Bread

Cornell diet bread is a bread that was engineered by Cornell University in 1946 to be as healthy as possible for people. It is excellent for people who are following a high protein diet. If you don't have miso, substitute it with concentrated fruit juice. This bread is low-rising and considered to have more nutrition than many other loaves of bread. It uses some less traditional ingredients that may be harder to find.

Ingredients:

- 1.5 cups water/ milk
- .33 cup soy flour
- 2.5 teaspoons yeast
- 4 cups whole wheat flour
- 2 tablespoons honey
- .33 cup nonfat dry milk
- 2 tablespoons miso
- 3 tablespoons vital gluten (optional)
- 3 tablespoons wheat germ

Instructions:

Proof the yeast in the water/ and milk with the honey. Add the miso and nonfat dry milk to the yeast mixture. Then add the wheat germ and vital gluten. Finally, add the soy flour and the whole wheat flour until you get the desired dough texture. After kneading for ten minutes, allow your dough to rise for an hour. Shape the dough into loaves after a second kneading, and you should wait for it to rise until it rises a bit more (around half an hour to an hour). For thirty to thirty-five minutes, bake at 400 degrees.

Mexican Cornbread

This cornbread will add spiciness to your life that will leave you satisfied. If you're feeling adventurous, you can add jalapenos for an extra kick. It's has a myriad of flavors, so it will not disappoint those who like trying new things.

Ingredients:

- .5 cup grated mild cheddar cheese
- .5 cup salsa
- 3 tablespoons vital gluten (optional)
- 2.5 teaspoons yeast
- .5 teaspoon salt
- 1.5 cups creamed corn
- 1 cup cornmeal
- 2 tablespoons fruit concentrate
- 2 tablespoons honey
- 4 cups whole wheat flour

Instructions:

Proof the yeast with the honey and fruit juice concentrate. Sift together dry ingredients. Mix all the outstanding ingredients into a bowl with the yeast mixture. Once the batter is mixed, you can put it directly in the pan and let it sit for twenty minutes while the oven is preheating. For twenty-eight to thirty-three minutes, bake at 350 degrees. It will pass the cake test and look golden on the top when it is done.

Rye and Pumpernickel

Rye bread is a type of whole grain bread that is made from rye flour and rye grains. Pumpernickel is a hearty variety of rye bread, which is usually darker, more flavorful, and a little sweeter than your traditional rye bread. Both are usually very grainy and are made into loaves often. There are light, medium, and dark version of rye bread that have varying combinations of grains. These breads are made sometimes by using a sourdough starter. To get that darker color, rye and pumpernickel breads may include cocoa powder, molasses, or coffee, which also enrich the flavors. These breads are great options if you're looking to try something different and a denser, darker bread.

NYC Rye

This fantastic rye bread is just like the bread you'd find in New York City. You're sure to love this bread, and it has less than ten ingredients, meaning that it won't take too much effort or money to replicate this classic New York bread. This is one of my favorite rye breads.

Ingredients:

- .25 cup nonfat dry milk
- 1.33 cups vegetable oil

- 1 cup and 2 tablespoons water
- 1 teaspoon salt
- 2.5 teaspoons yeast
- 2 .33 cups white flour
- 2 teaspoons caraway seeds
- 2 tablespoons honey
- 1.33 cups rye flour

Instructions:

In the sugar, honey, and oil, proof the yeast. When the yeast is proofed, add the salt, caraway seeds, and dry milk. Then, incorporate the flours. When the dough is a nice texture for kneading, knead the dough for ten minutes and then let it rest in the bowl so it can rise for about an hour. When the dough is puffy, push it down gently in the bowl and knead it for a few minutes before rolling it out into loaves. Settle it into a greased pan and let it rise until the dough is a little bit above the top of the pan, which can take up to an hour and a half. Cook in a 350-degree oven for around thirty to thirty-eight minutes or until it reaches the internal temperature of 200 degrees.

Salted Rye Bread

For those of you who love a bit of salt, this recipe can be a great choice for you. This recipe makes a large amount of bread, and you should get two big braided loaves from it.

Ingredients:

- 1 tablespoon cold water
- 1 egg white, beaten
- 2 cups unsifted rye flour
- 1 tablespoon caraway
- 1 tablespoon salt
- 1 tablespoon butter
- 5 cups unsifted white flour
- 2.5 cups warm water
- 6 teaspoons yeast

Instructions:

Mix both flours. Then, in a large container, blend three cups of the flour mixture with the caraway, salt, and yeast. Slowly, add the warm water to the dry ingredients. Mix for two minutes. Add half of the caraway mixture to the dry ingredient mixture until the batter becomes thick. Stir in the rest of the mixture to make a soft dough. Knead the dough for ten minutes until it is elastic and smooth. Then, let it rest in a greased bowl until it has doubled, which takes around forty-five minutes. When risen, divide the dough into two pieces, and then for each half, create three eighteen-inch ropes. Braid these three ropes together for each loaf. Let the bread rise for thirty minutes more. At 450 degrees, bake for twenty minutes. If you'd like, and I suggest that you do, sprinkle the loaves with coarse salt and bake for five additional minutes.

Nutty Wheat Rye

This rye bread will have a fantastic nutty texture and can be customized based on what nuts you like best. I suggest walnuts. Nuts like brazil nuts or hazelnuts are unique choices that will give this bread a special flavor.

Ingredients:

- .25 cup walnut oil
- 1.5 cups water/ milk
- 1.33 teaspoons sugar
- 1.33 teaspoons salt
- 1 cup whole wheat flour
- 2.5 teaspoons yeast
- 2 cups white flour
- 1 cup rye flour

Instructions:

Proof your yeast in your water/milk and sugar. When the yeast is proofed, add the other ingredients, saving the flours for last. Mix until well incorporated. Knead the dough if not using a mixer for around five to ten minutes or until elastic. After the dough has sat for around an hour, punch the dough down, and you should knead briefly before shaping. Shape your bread and place it on a greased pan. Let it risk for at least another half an hour—Bake at 450 for around thirty minutes.

Mustard Rye

Mustard rye bread is a moist bread that will smell great when you are baking it. This one has more ingredients than most of the breads in this book, but it is well worth the effort you put in. If you want a unique bread, this is a good choice, and it's sure to impress anyone who you serve it too. You can't go wrong with this combination of grains and mustard.

Ingredients:

- 1.5 cups water
- 1 cup rye flour
- 2 eggs
- 2 tablespoons mustard
- 4 cups whole wheat flour
- 2.5 teaspoons of yeast
- 1.33 tablespoons vegetable oil
- 1 teaspoon mustard seeds
- 2 tablespoons honey
- 3 tablespoons vital gluten (optional)
- 2 teaspoons caraway (optional)
- 1 teaspoon salt

Instructions:

Proof the yeast in the water and honey. Add all other ingredients, adding the flours last once the other ingredients have merged. Knead your dough as necessary then let it rise for ten to fifteen minutes. Flatten the dough on a counter and knead it some more by folding it towards you. Shape your bread and then put it on your baking sheet. Let the shaped bread rise for twenty minutes as the oven preheats. Then, make three diagonal slashes before putting the bread into the oven. Before it goes into the oven, I suggest that you brush the top of the bread with water to create an ideal crust— Bake at 400 degrees for twenty to twenty-five minutes. When you take it out of the oven, take it off from the baking sheet to set on a metal rack.

Classic Pumpernickel

This recipe is ideal if you want to make a classic loaf of pumpernickel bread. It has a strong grainy flavor that feels quite decadent. This bread is perfect for sandwiches or toasting.

Ingredients:

- 1.33 tablespoons caraway seeds
- 1 cup rye flour
- 2 tablespoons vegetable oil
- 3.33 cups whole wheat flour
- 2.5 teaspoons yeast
- .66 cups black bean flakes
- 2 teaspoons baking soda
- 2 cups water
- .5 teaspoon salt
- 4 tablespoons molasses
- 3 tablespoons vital gluten

Instructions:

Proof the yeast with your water and molasses. Once the yeast is bubbly, mix in all the other ingredients in the order of the list. Knead the dough before letting it sit until it nearly doubles. Push the dough down and knead again before shaping the dough and placing it on greased cookware. Let rise once more. When it has puffed up, bake it in a 375-degree oven for about fifty-five minutes or until the temperature reaches 200 degrees in the middle.

Light Pumpernickel

This pumpernickel still has a powerful taste but in a lighter color than darker pumpernickel bread recipes. It has a bit of cocoa powder in it to balance the flavors and give this recipe a little something extra.

Ingredients:

- 2.5 teaspoons yeast
- 1 teaspoon salt
- 2 cups rye flour
- 3 tablespoons vegetable oil
- 2.5 teaspoons caraway seed
- 3 tablespoons unsweetened cocoa powder
- 2.5 cups white flour
- 1.5 cups water
- 2 tablespoons sugar
- 3 tablespoons molasses

Instructions:

Begin by proofing your yeast in the water and sugar. Add the ingredients as listed and gradually add the flour. Knead the bread, let it rise, punch it down, shape it how you wish, let it rise again, and cook it at 375 degrees from around fifty minutes to one hour until the bread starts to get crustier.

Dark Pumpernickel

This recipe is similar to the light pumpernickel, but it is darker, and it used instant coffee to darken it and give the sweetness of the molasses a contrasting flavor, which adds depth to this bread. This one also has cocoa powder!

Ingredients:

- 2.5 teaspoons yeast
- 1.33 tablespoons instant coffee granules
- 2.5 teaspoons caraway seed
- 2 cups white flour
- 1 cup rye flour
- 1 cup whole wheat flour
- 1.33 cups water
- 1.33 tablespoons brown sugar
- .25 cup molasses
- 1.33 teaspoons salt
- 2.66 tablespoons vegetable oil
- 2 tablespoons unsweetened cocoa powder

Instructions:

In sugar and water, proof your yeast. Then, add the remaining ingredients, leaving the flour for last. Mix in the flour until the dough doesn't cling to the sides of the bowl. The dough should be in a ball. Knead until it becomes smooth and stretchy, then wait for it to rise for about an hour. Push the dough down in the bowl, and then scrape it out and shape it into loaves. Let it rise for half an hour more than bake in the oven for around one hour.

CHAPTER 5: THE GREAT SOURDOUGH

What is Sourdough?

One of the most intimidating breads of all is sourdough, but don't run away from these recipes because it's not as arduous and laborious as you may assume. With some simple instructions, all your worries and doubts about making this bread will be relieved. This bread is great for people with diabetes because the glycemic index is lower than it is in yeast breads. It's also better for your digestive system, and those with IBS may benefit from eating this bread. Some research has shown that it is good for weight loss. Additionally, it has lots of folate and antioxidants that can help your health, including helping you to be more resistant to certain cancers. Thus, it has several worthwhile health benefits while tasting great.

Sourdough is a special kind of bread that uses the bacteria in the flour for fermentation rather than relying on yeast. It's rumored that this bread was first created after people left unleavened bread dough out, and in time, wild yeast started to grow, causing leavening qualities. While the origins of this bread aren't known for sure, sourdough bread is undoubtedly unique. This bread is slightly more sour than other breads and has the same kind of tartness as sour cream as yogurt. It is not tart in the same way of sour candy, but it does have that extra something that other breads are lacking. The sourness comes from the chemical process created because of the fermentation of the flour and water.

Sourdough is known for having recipes that are very minimal despite having a reputation for being complicated. Many sourdough recipes can just have the starter, flour, and salt, making this kind of bread shockingly simple. Some recipes are more elaborate, but traditionally, sourdough doesn't make the recipe more complex than it needs to be. There are some complicated sourdough recipes out there. With some light TLC, sourdough will respond well to your efforts.

The perks of sourdough are that while there's a lot of waiting time, you'll only have about fifteen minutes of active work in some recipes, which is even less than many other breads, and sourdough is sure to impress all the people in your life. As you wait for the sourdough to be ready, you can do other things because you don't have to monitor the bread during the entire process. Many people believe that sourdough is finicky and requires you to time each step perfectly, but most people should be able to make the fermentation time and rising time work with their schedule because you can tweak the recipe to work with your needs.

One concern that people have is that sourdough starter is hard to maintain, which can be true if you aren't aware of how to store it. People too often think that the starter will die if they don't add to it daily or use it regularly, but the truth is that once you get it started, it can be stored in the fridge for months. With proper storage, maintenance for sourdough bread is low. The more you learn about storing sourdough, the less you'll worry about the effort required to maintain it.

People also mistakenly worry that sourdough is expensive to make, but it mainly uses cheap flour, water, and salt, all of which are incredibly inexpensive. While expensive flours can be used to make sourdough, whatever flour you have will work if given time. Thus, you can make a loaf for less than a dollar, so while sourdough is more expensive in stores, the biggest cost you'll pay for making your own sourdough is the effort to learn how to do it, which doesn't have to be a tedious process if you allow it to be satisfying and fun rather than looking at it like it is a chore.

I will admit that sourdough will probably be trickier for you to get the hang of than other breads in this book, but only because there's more to learn. However, when you know the process, you'll learn that it isn't that complicated after all, and with practice, you may find that it's your new favorite bread to make! It can also be one of the cheapest too, depending on what you put in it. Using the recipes provided, give sourdough a chance because it will be a major accomplishment when you make your first sourdough loaf.

Sourdough Starter

Sourdough starter isn't complex at all. Time-consuming, yes, but complex, definitely not. In short, it is just flour and water, so making your own sourdough starter won't require a lot of ingredients. Mostly, it will require time, but it won't be an active time that you have to invest. Most of the time, your sourdough starter will be sitting around waiting or growth. Thus, you won't have t0 put in hours of hard labor just to create the starter. A few minutes for around a week, maybe all the time, you need to prepare your starter. Once it is prepared, you can maintain it so that you don't have to start from scratch again.

While making a sourdough starter is a rewarding skill to learn, if you aren't up for making the sourdough starter yourself, you can buy premade sourdough starter to make your job easier and cut through some of the hardship. From there, all you have to do is add it to your recipe and get baking. It couldn't be any easier than using a premade starter, but making your own takes just a little bit of extra time and knowledge, so I recommend that you make your own.

Making Sourdough Starter

If you want to make your sourdough starter, you are going to have to wait several days or even weeks before you can make bread, and it takes months before the starter has fully matured and the flavors have fully developed. Nevertheless, your patience can pay off once you have your starter created.

To make your sourdough starter, all you will need is water and flour. You can use whatever flour you prefer in this process (though some work better than others). Begin your starter with one cup of flour and then an additional half a cup of water. The water should be cool, not to disturb the yeast. Put these ingredients in a container, such as a glass jar. It should be one quart or larger to allow room for growth. Mix the ingredients and ensure that the flour is fully incorporated. Keep the mix on your counter in a room temperature environment for one day.

After twenty-four hours, you may start to see the starter bubbling and having growth, but it's okay if you don't see that yet. Get rid of half of the starter and add a cup of flour and half a cup of cool water. Again, you should mix it and store it at room temperature for one day. On day three, you should see more activity, and you'll have to start "feeding" your sourdough starter twice a day. With each feeding, you should repeat the process of weighing 113 grams of starter and discarding it and then adding your single cup of flour and your half a cup of water. Continue this process through the fifth day. By day five, it will have more bubbles and "gullies." It should smell a bit sour but not too much so. If it hasn't done that, try the feeding process for a few more days. When it is ready, feed it one last time and then let it sit for six to eight hours. From there, your starter should be ready to use. You can then store it or make bread with it. Continue storing it and feeding it when necessary to mature it.

While you can use any flour that you want to begin the starter, whole grain flours are more likely to create success because of the environment that whole wheat flour is in. All-purpose flour can work, but sometimes it will take longer for this starter to develop.

Regarding the temperature of your home, a temperature above sixty-eight degrees is preferable. If your house is colder than that, you may need to adjust. Try to find a warmer place to put your starter, such as on top of the fridge. Don't put it somewhere too warm (like on top of the oven while it is on).

If it takes longer to start your starter, don't fear. Some people have reported their starters taking up to three weeks for their starter to get going. Thus, you should be patient because if you are, you will eventually have results.

There are plenty of other recipes you can find on the internet, and many people use different methods for their sourdough starters, but I find this one to be straight forward and easy to accomplish for even beginner sourdough makers. With minimal time and a week of waiting, you can be well on your way to making sourdough.

Storing Your Starter

The first place that you can store your sourdough starter is in your fridge. This method is common and is to be used if you don't plan on using your starter frequently. To store your starter in this manner, feed your starter to start the process and then put it in an airtight container, preferably one that is glass. Do not fill it to the brim because the starter needs room to grow. Place the jar in the part of your fridge that is coldest, which is often the top shelf. If your starter is at least three months old, you can leave it untouched in your fridge for around two months. After that time, you will need to nourish your ravenous sourdough starter and return it to the fridge. When you want to use it, you should feed the starter, leave it out of the fridge for about twelve hours until it starts to have growth and gets bubbly.

A second method you can use to store your sourdough starter is to put it in the freezer. You begin this process by feeding your starter. Then, when you start to see the bubbles in the starter, you put it into the freezer in a freezer-safe container. When you want to use it, you'll have to put it in the fridge for a day before feeding it again once it has thawed. After feeding it a few times, you should start to see the bubbliness yet again, at which point you can use it. This is a low maintenance method. It's easy to reactivate this starter after taking it from the freezer. The risk of freezer burn is the main downside of this method, but if you store it well, this risk is greatly reduced. It may also become less active when in the freezer for a long time (as normal yeast does as well).

The final method for storing your sourdough starter is meant for storing starter for a long time. It will keep for an indefinite time and is good if you want back up the starter for times when your main starter doesn't work how you intend. You can do this by feeding your starter until it bubbles. After it has been reactivated, you should pour it on parchment paper in a slim sheet. It will air dry in around one day. If your layer is thicker, it may take longer, so aim to make it as thin as you can. When it is dry, you can peel it off the parchment paper and break it into smaller pieces. Alternatively, you can grind it into a powder. When it is into pieces, put it into an airtight container and store it somewhere that is cool and dark. You can also put it in the freezer if you wish. This starter will last for years. To reconstitute it, you will have to weigh how much dried starter you want you to use and use the same weight of water. Leave it covered with a cloth for several hours until it starts to activate, and you see bubbles. Once it is activated, you are good to bake with it. If you use sourdough starter frequently, it is not worth the effort, but for those who want to always have some around, this method can be ideal.

Making Sour Dough

Making sourdough doesn't have to be a painful experience. To make it easier, it is usually recommended that you use a Dutch oven, but you may also another heavy pot that has a lid. The Dutch oven method helps to keep the moisture levels balanced, which can be hard to regulate using your oven alone. However, in a pinch, you can use just a cookie sheet, but you need to be sure to, at the very least, steam your bread and cover it with some tented foil until you are directed to take the lid off.

For all the recipes, you will follow the same basic instructions for baking the bread. While some methods are shorter, and you can easily use those methods, this method provides better, more consistent bread, which is why I've chosen it for this book.

You will start by ensuring that you have taken out your sourdough starter and that you have fed it until it is incredibly active. About eight to twelve hours before you make your bread, you should place all the leavening ingredients (1/2 cup of your flour, and half of your water or milk) into a bowl and mix them. When this step is complete, the mix you've made should be able to float or bobble in water.

Then, you may add any of the fluid that remains and the salt with the leavening mix. From there, you can add any other ingredients except for the flour, which you should slowly incorporate last. Cover the dough and let it rest for a minimum of at least thirty minutes, but many people may choose to wait even up to four hours. Knead the dough for four rotations every thirty minutes until you've repeated this process six times. If you have less time, you can reduce the number of times that you knead, but that is not ideal. In any case, be sure that your dough starts to get elastic and no longer feels as wet as it was before.

When the dough has been kneaded, let it rest for another hour. Don't fret if yours doesn't puff as much as other breads do. That is normal. Once your bread has risen a bit, you can break your dough into two rounds. Let your dough rest for half an hour, and then do the final shaping of your dough, and put the loaves into containers (you can transfer them to a Dutch oven just before you cook them). Then, let your dough rest and let it rise overnight (in the fridge up to fifteen hours) or for a minimum of three to four hours (at room temperature). Again, the bread should puff up during this time, which tells you that it is time to get in the oven.

Heat your oven to around 500 degrees (or as high as your oven will go if it doesn't go that high) and put in your empty Dutch ovens (if you only have one Dutch oven, you can bake the loaves back to back Store your other loaf in the fridge as you wait). Take out the Dutch oven after thirty minutes and take off the lid and put your first loaf into the Dutch oven. Then, score the crown of the bread, and put it covered in the oven for twenty minutes. After twenty minutes (or slightly more if your oven temperature is lower), bring the oven temperature down to 450 degrees and let the bread bake for an additional ten minutes. Once the ten minutes have passed, you can bake the bread uncovered until it is starting to get golden and then a deeper brown, which will take around an additional thirty to fifty minutes. If you want to be more precise with your cooking, you can use a thermometer. When it is done, the internal temperature of bread will be between 190 degrees and 200 degrees.

When your sourdough is done, you can lift it from the Dutch oven and should let it cool entirely before cutting and serving. Once you have cooked your first loaf, if you need to cook a second loaf, you can cook the second loaf immediately after in your Dutch oven without having to re-preheat the Dutch oven because it will still be hot enough.

Basic Sourdough

If you want a basic sourdough that has lots of strong flavors, this recipe is a great choice for you. It is reminiscent of San Francisco's sourdough.

Ingredients:

- .75 cup milk
- 2.5 teaspoons yeast
- 2.5 tablespoons shortening
- 1.5 cups sourdough starter
- 1.33 tablespoons salt
- 2.5 tablespoons sugar
- 4 cups flour

Instructions:

This is a quintessential sourdough recipe, so follow the basic sourdough steps, and you should be good to go.

Easy Wheat Sourdough

For those of you who want wheat sourdough rather than white, this wheat sourdough is another easy recipe for those who don't have much experience with sourdough. This recipe has the same level of flavor as classic white sourdough but with the perks of wheat flour. This dough requires more salt than most bread, so don't worry about how much is included. It's mostly the same as the white sourdough except that its flour ratio is different.

Ingredients:

- .75 cup milk
- 1.5 cups sourdough starter
- 1.33 tablespoons salt
- 2.5 tablespoons shortening
- 2.5 cups flour
- 2.5 teaspoons yeast
- 2.33 tablespoons sugar
- 1.5 cups whole wheat flour

Instructions:

There are no special instructions for this one, so just follow the normal baking style of sourdough, and you should excel at baking this bread!

French Sourdough

If you like French bread and you like sourdough, this bread may worm its way into your heart. It's perfect for sandwiches or just eating with a meal. I love French bread, so this recipe is a must-have for me. It's also a nice recipe because the ingredients are basic, and it requires no special instructions.

Ingredients:

- 1.33 cups starter
- 1.33 teaspoons salt
- 2 teaspoons sugar
- 2.5 teaspoons yeast
- .75 cup water
- 4 cups flour

Instructions:

Use normal sourdough instructions.

Pumpernickel Sourdough

As I've mentioned before, some pumpernickel breads are also often sourdough breads. These two types blend nicely to make an irresistible bread, and this recipe even has a bit of cocoa powder in it, which is the secret ingredient you didn't know you needed! This is one of the heartiest loaves of bread in the book, and it feels so luxurious.

Ingredients:

- .25 cup molasses
- 1 cup starter
- 3 tablespoons vital gluten (optional)
- 2 tablespoons unsweetened cocoa powder
- 1 tablespoon caraway seeds (optional)
- 1 teaspoon salt
- 3.5 cups whole wheat flour
- 2.5 teaspoons yeast
- 1 cup rye flour
- 2 tablespoons vegetable oil

Instructions:

Stick to the normal sourdough instructions, and it may help to know that this bread has a low to medium rise, meaning it will not puff out as much as some other breeds, so don't worry if it's slow to rise. This bread will have a dark, rich color.

Maple & Walnut Sourdough

If you're feeling ambitious, this multigrain sourdough hits the spot and reimagines traditional sourdough recipes. It feels especially artisan, and you'll no doubt feel proud when you're able to make this beautiful bread.

Ingredients:

- .25 cup maple syrup
- 2 teaspoons yeast
- .25 cup raisins (optional)
- 3 tbs spoons vital gluten (optional)
- .25 cup walnuts (chopped)
- .25 teaspoon cinnamon (optional)
- 1 cup sourdough starter
- 2 eggs
- .75 cup milk or water
- 1 teaspoon salt
- 4.5 cups whole wheat flour

Instructions:

Follow the basic sourdough instructions, and you should note that this bread will rise to about ¾ of your baking dish.

CHAPTER 6: PIZZA AND FLATBREAD

Pizza

Pizza has a long history, and the styles of pizza can be divisive. The flatbread now attributed to Italy, <u>focaccia</u> is often seen as a precursor to the pizza that we know today, which the Romans started making in antiquity. It wasn't until around the eighteenth century that Italians began crafting the pizza we know currently in Naples; however, the word pizza has been used since the year 997. Pizza became a worldwide staple after World War II when soldiers discovered the wonders of pizza and brought it home with them. Ever since then, cities in the United States like New York and Chicago have all created their signature styles of pizza that have distinct characteristics.

Let your dough rise based on how thick you want the crust. For thin crusts, don't allow any rise time while for thicker crusts, allow thirty minutes of rising time. If you want to keep the crust soft, put olive oil on the crust once it comes out of the oven. Or if you plan on using many topping, brush the dough with oil before you bake it. Putting the toppings towards the outside of the pizza rather than on the inside will ensure that the middle cooks all the way through. These tips should help you ensure quality pizza, but practice will be the best tool to make your pizza perfect.

Classic Pizza Dough

If you're craving a recipe that tastes the most average pizza that's made commercially, this is the dough for you. You can make two mid-sized or one large pizza with this recipe. It's one of my favorites!

Ingredients:

- 2.5 teaspoons yeast
- 3.5 cups flour
- 1 tablespoon olive oil
- 2 teaspoons salt
- 1.25 cups warm water
- 2 teaspoons sugar

Instructions:

Proof the yeast in the water and the sugar. Let this mixture sit for around five minutes. It should get bubbly. Then, you can incorporate the salt, oil, and one cup of the flour. Add the remaining flour gradually after the first cup is mixed in. You may need to add extra flour to get a texture that is stiff but not sticky. Knead for five minutes before placing in an oiled bowl to rise for approximately an hour, at which point it should've doubled in size. When it has doubled, punch the dough down and roll it out before placing it on a greased pan. Bake the topped pizza for fifteen to twenty minutes at 425 degrees.

Dreamy, Easy Pizza Dough

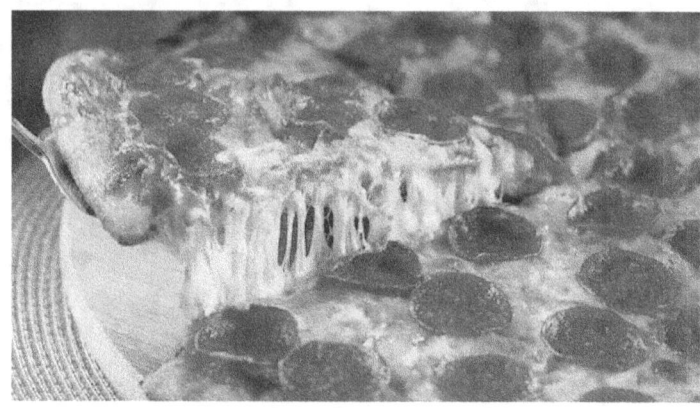

Sometimes you just want an ordinary pizza crust, and if that's the case, this dough is for you. It's as basic as a pizza crust can get while still maintain a great flavor. Making your own pizza dough seems impressive, but it is deceptively easy. The perk of this pizza dough is that you don't have to let it rise.

Ingredients:

- 1 teaspoon sugar
- 1 teaspoon salt
- 2.5 cups flour
- 2.5 teaspoons yeast
- 1 cup warm water
- 2 tablespoons olive oil

Instructions:

To begin making this pizza, turn on your oven to 450 degrees. For the dough, start by proofing your yeast in the water and sugar. Wait five minutes for the yeast to ferment. When the yeast is ready, add the salt and olive oil and mix. Then, incorporate the flour until you get a ball. Knead for five minutes before rolling out your dough in your desired shape. For me, it is often easiest to make square pizza and press the dough out onto a greased cookie sheet with a one-inch edge, but you can use any greased pan you want, including specialty pizza pans. Be sure to shape the crust to your desired thickness. Put the pizza in the oven for five minutes without any toppings. Then, take it out and add the toppings before baking for another fifteen to twenty-five minutes or until it starts to get a crispy crust. It should cool for five minutes before you cut it and serve it.

Whole Wheat Pizza Dough

For those who want a healthier version of pizza, this whole wheat dough is perfect for you. This dough is still simple, but it has the added benefit of a whole wheat crust. This pizza is 100% whole wheat, so it is packed full of nutrients and will leave you feeling full even after just one slice!

Ingredients:

- .75 cup warm water
- 2 teaspoons yeast
- 1 tablespoon vital gluten
- 1 teaspoon sugar
- .5 teaspoon salt
- 2 cups whole wheat flour
- 2 tablespoons olive oil

Instructions:

Proof the yeast in the water and the sugar. Then, mix in all the other ingredients, saving the flour for last. Knead for ten minutes, then allow the bread to sit in the bowl so that it can rise. Preheat the oven at 450 degrees as the dough rests for thirty minutes. Roll out your dough and spread it into your pizza pan. From there, you can put the toppings on and bake your pizza for fifteen to twenty-five minutes. It will be done when the edges crisp, and the cheese in the middle starts to bubble. Wait the required five minutes before serving and then enjoy it! For a lighter taste, you can use half all-purpose flour instead of all whole wheat.

Chicago Deep Dish Dough

Based on a pizza-making style that developed in Chicago, deep-dish pizza has a high crust that looks like a wall around the pizza; therefore, this kind of pizza contains a lot of sauce and cheese, making it distinct. Many people love this pizza, and it's certainly an original experience if you have never tried it before. Using cornmeal is the trick to making this pizza perfect. This pizza will require 9x2 inch round pans to shape the crust into. This recipe will make one or two crusts, depending on how thick you want the crust to be.

Ingredients:

- ½ teaspoon salt
- 3 cups flour

- 1 cup warm water
- 1/3 cup cornmeal
- 1.5 teaspoon yeast
- 2 tablespoons olive oil (for coating)
- 2 tablespoons olive oil
- 1 teaspoon sugar

Instructions:

Begin this recipe by dissolving the yeast in the sugar. Add in the olive oil, salt, and cornmeal. Then, incorporate the flour until a ball of dough is formed. Knead for ten minutes. Then, coat the dough ball with the additional olive oil and let rest in a bowl for one or two hours. Using a floured service, push down your dough and form it into a rectangle, flour it, and then allow it to rise for an hour in the fridge. Roll out your dough again to the size you need it and place it in the pan. Add your desired pizza sauce and toppings. For twenty to twenty-eight minutes, bake at 425 degrees.

Thin Crust Brioche Dough

Brioche is a French pastry bread with a slight sweetness that can be made to make a myriad of recipes. This brioche pizza dough is a little sweeter than most pizza doughs, but it will taste decadent and complement any sauce well. This is the richest pizza dough in this book, and it has an ideal softness. If you serve this to guests, they are sure to rave about it.

Ingredients:

- .5 cup lukewarm milk
- 1 teaspoon yeast
- 2 tablespoons butter, melted and let cool to a lukewarm temperature
- 2 tablespoons sugar
- 3 cups flour
- 2 eggs
- .5 teaspoon salt

Instructions:

Proof the yeast in the milk with the sugar in a large bowl. After five minutes, add the salt, butter, and eggs. Once the mix is well mixed, add the flour gradually until the dough forms into a ball. Knead for five minutes. Let the dough rise once, for about thirty minutes, before kneading it shortly. Stretch this dough yourself to place it in a very greased pan rather than rolling it out with a rolling pin. Add the toppings as you normally would. At 350 degrees, cook the pizza for thirty to forty minutes until the cheese starts to bubble and the crust is golden.

Spicy Corn Pizza Dough

This is a recipe with a little kick, and I love it because it adds a unique twist to the basic pizza dough that we all know and love. If you like spicy foods, you cannot go wrong with this pizza dough because it makes pizza even more interesting. It used cornmeal to give it its texture. If you want a corn dough without the spice, leave out the jalapenos and red pepper flakes altogether.

Ingredients:

- .25 teaspoon salt
- .5 cup cornmeal
- 1.5 cups flour
- 1 tablespoon oil (preferably corn or vegetable)
- 1 teaspoon dried red pepper flakes (you can add or subtract some for your desired heat level)
- 1 teaspoon yeast
- 1-2 diced jalapenos
- .66 cup warm water

Instructions:

Proof your yeast in water for five minutes. Mix in the salt, oil, and cornmeal to the yeast blend and stir thoroughly before adding the remaining ingredients, saving the flour for last. Knead for five minutes before letting the dough rest for around twenty minutes. After twenty minutes, you can knead the dough once more before rolling it out to fit your pan. You may have to press some of the jalapenos back into the dough after rolling. Add your toppings, and you should bake your pizza for fifteen to twenty-five minutes at 450 degrees or until the cheese starts to bubble, and the crust is golden.

Thin Crusted Sourdough

For those of you who have an interest in sourdough bread, this pizza crust tastes excellent and gives you the added challenge of having to use your sourdough starter. If you're a fan of sourdough bread, this pizza crust may be your new favorite. Test your sourdough skills with this amazing pizza dough recipe. It's not that hard at all.

Ingredients:

- .25 teaspoon salt
- 2 cups flour
- 1 tablespoon olive oil
- 1 tablespoon of water (if needed)
- 1 cup sourdough starter
- 1 teaspoon yeast

Instructions:

Begin by mixing your yeast with your prepared sourdough starter. Then, incorporate the olive oil and the salt. Finally, add the flour. Knead the dough for five minutes before coating with oil and allowing it to rest for thirty minutes. After thirty minutes, you can roll out the dough and place it unto a greased pan before topping and baking your pizza at 425 degrees for twenty to twenty-five minutes or until it starts to get bubbly in the middle and the crust is browned. Let it cool before you cut it and serve it.

Flatbread

Flatbread is a type of bread that is rolled and flattened before cooking. These breads are often unleavened, but some may be leavened. Most cultures have a type of this bread, but they each have their unique variations, so you can try them all. Here are just some of the varieties that you can find around the world.

Pita

Pita is a round flatbread that is slightly leavened to give it an airy taste. It is often found in the Mediterranean and the Middle East, but it can be enjoyed everywhere. When you buy pita at the store, it often lacks freshness because it has been sitting for multiple days. Thus, making your own pita can give you unparalleled freshness. This recipe will make eight pieces of pita, and you'd benefit from having a cast-iron pan.

Ingredients:

- .25 cup whole wheat flour
- 2.5 cups all-purpose flour
- 1 teaspoon kosher salt
- .5 teaspoon sugar
- 1 cup lukewarm water
- 2 tablespoons olive oil

- 2 teaspoons yeast

Instructions:

Begin by dissolving yeast and sugar in the warm water. Then, combine this mix with the whole wheat flour and ¼ cup flour. Let this mix sit for around fifteen minutes until it becomes foamy. Add the other ingredients, saving the rest of the flour for last. Stir until the ingredients are roughly incorporated and then knead for one or two minutes. Knead for another two minutes on a floured surface until elastic. Let the dough rest for ten minutes before kneading again for another two minutes. Wait for the dough to double in size, which will take around an hour. Let the oven preheat to 475 degrees and put a large cast-iron pan on the lowest rack of the oven. Form eight balls of dough and let rest for ten more minutes. Press one ball down into a disk and roll into a circle with an eight-inch diameter. Place it on your hot skilled for two minutes and then flip so that it cooks another minute. It should come out looking mostly pale with a few brown spots. Repeat this process with all your pieces of pita.

Focaccia

Focaccia is an Italian flatbread that is essentially a pizza without the pizza toppings. It is topped with herbs that make it delectable. Further, the dough itself only has six ingredients, making it an excellent starter. I recommend adding herbs such as garlic and rosemary! This dish is good fresh out of the oven or served at room temperature, so no matter how you eat it, you'll fall in love with the texture and the flavors of this dish.

Ingredients:

- .25 cup olive oil
- 2 teaspoons sugar
- 1 tablespoon salt
- 2 teaspoons yeast
- 4.5 cups flour
- 2 cups warm water

For the topping:

- 4 tablespoons fresh herbs or 2 tablespoons dry herbs (such as rosemary, basil, and thyme).
- 2 minced garlic cloves
- 5 tablespoons olive oil
- A bit of salt and hand-ground pepper

Instructions:

Proof the yeast by putting it into the water and the sugar. Allow this blend to sit for five minutes and then mix in the water, olive oil, and half the flour. Then, gradually add the rest of the flour. Mix and for four minutes, knead the dough. Add more flour if the dough is too gooey. When you prod at the dough with your finger, and it slowly comes back, that's when your dough has been kneaded enough. Let the dough rest for around two or three hours or until it has doubled. Grease a 12x17 inch baking pan with sides that are one inch tall. Use a decent amount of olive oil in this process. Don't be stingy! Punch the dough down and stretch into your pan. Let it rest for up to ten minutes and then stretch further into the corners of the pan if you experience shrinkage. Put the pan in the fridge for one hour and up to twenty-four hours. It develops flavor as it sits longer, so if you can afford the extra time, aim for at least twelve hours of resting. Take the dough out to a room-temperature environment as you preheat the oven for around twenty minutes. Mix the toppings you want to use. Then, dimple your dough with your fingers before spreading the herb mixture. The dough should be fully covered with oil, so add more if you need to. Sprinkle the dough with pepper and salt. Bake the dough until it starts to become golden for twenty to twenty-three minutes. You can eat it hot or at room temperature.

Naan

Naan is one of the flatbreads that is leavened, which adds a nice puffiness to this bread, which gives it a light texture. Naan is commonly eaten in India, and it is often made in a tandoor, a clay oven, but you can enjoy this bread in the comfort of your own home by using a heated iron skillet. This recipe will yield 6 naans, so you may want to double it if you are serving a lot of people, especially with how good this recipe will taste. You'll be wanting more as soon as you finish your batch!

Ingredients:

- .5 teaspoon of anise seeds (optional)
- 1 teaspoon salt
- .75 cup warm water
- 1 tablespoon fresh parsley (optional) for serving
- 1 teaspoon instant yeast
- 2 cups flour
- 2 tablespoons butter for brushing on top of the naans
- 3 tablespoons plain yogurt
- 2 tablespoons olive oil
- 3 teaspoons sugar

Instructions:

Start by mixing the yeast, sugar, salt, flour, and anise seeds in a big bowl. In a different bowl, add the yogurt, olive oil, and warm water. Whisk the ingredients together. Add the yogurt blend to the big bowl with the dry ingredients; knead the dough until it comes together. Do not over-knead it. Let the dough rest for one to two hours. It should be twice its original size. Take the dough out and roll it out into a rectangle. Cut it into six pieces, ball the pieces back up, and sprinkle each piece with flour to avoid it sticking. Heat your cast-iron skillet or another heavy non-stick pan until it is as incredibly hot. Roll the pieces out with a rolling pin and brush the dough off so that it doesn't have too much flour on it. Cook the pieces in the skillet until the dough starts to get bubbles and is golden on the bottom. Turn the dough and cook the other side for around a couple minutes. When the naan is done, take it off the skillet and brush with the melted butter. Cook the other naans until they are all done. You may have to lower the heat as you continue, so keep a careful watch on your heat levels. If you wish, sprinkle with parsley when you're done. Then, you're free to enjoy your naan!

Flour Tortilla

Flour tortillas are a flatbread that I'm sure you're familiar with that originated in Mesoamerica by cultures such as the Aztecs. This is a flat, unleavened bread that is shaped into rounds. This recipe is one of the simplest that you'll find, but the flavors pack a punch, and you're sure to want to make these instead of buying your tortillas. This recipe will make around twelve eight-inch tortillas, but you should be warned that these will be devoured quickly.

Ingredients:

- .25 cup vegetable oil
- 1.5 teaspoons salt
- 4.25 cups all-purpose flour
- 1.75 cups hot water

Instructions:

Start by mixing the flour and salt. Then, mix in the water and the oil, mixing with your hands until you have formed a ball, and you get a soft, shapeable dough that shouldn't be sticky. If it is gooey, you can add more flour. Knead the dough ten times until the dough becomes elastic. Once kneaded, divide the dough into twelve balls and flatten them each slightly. Add flour to these disks and let them sit as you heat a nonstick pan using medium heat. Roll out a dough disk into an eight-inch circle and then cook for one minute before flipping and cooking the other side for thirty-seconds. You should see brown spots starting to appear. Repeat this process with the remaining tortilla discs until you are finished. Monitor your heat as you go to maintain even cooking temperatures.

Lavash

Lavash is an easy to make flatbread that won't take you too long to make. It is an unleavened flatbread that is often found in areas such as Western Asia, such as Turkey, Iran, and Azerbaijan. This oven-baked flatbread is great if you're looking to try new cuisines and expand your culinary horizons. It pairs well with most foods.

Ingredients:

- 1 egg
- 2.5 cups flour
- 1 teaspoon salt
- 5 tablespoons unsalted butter, melted and cooled a bit
- ½ teaspoon sugar
- .75 cup water

Instructions;

Start by putting the flour, salt, and sugar into a bowl and mix them until they are combined. Add in another bowl your water, egg, and half of your butter. Then, stir in the egg mix to the dry ingredients until the dough comes together. Add additional water if the dough doesn't have enough moisture. Knead the dough lightly, around five times. Then, divide the dough into three and allow it to sit for thirty minutes. Ready your oven by preheating it to 375 degrees, You will use the remaining butter to grease a pan. Roll each ball to 1/8-inch thickness and brush with butter or oil—Bake for ten to fifteen minutes. The crust will be golden when it is done. Repeat this process with the other two balls of dough.

Frybread

Frybread is a type of bread originated by Native Americans, meaning that there are many varieties of this type of bread because different tribes in different regions had their own variations. This recipe is one of the simplest versions of fry bread that doesn't include eggs and uses baking powder instead of yeast (for slight leavening). This is a perfect bread to serve with stew or to serve with honey or jam. This recipe makes four small frybread loaves, so you may want to double it.

Ingredients:

- 1.5 teaspoons baking powder
- 1 cup oil for frying
- .5 cup milk
- 1 cup flour

Instructions:

Prepare your ingredients and set them aside. Then, heat oil in an iron skillet or heavy saucepan until the oil reaches 350 degrees. While the oil heats, combine all your ingredients and mix them, adding the milk last. Knead a few times on a floured surface. When kneaded, split the dough into four pieces and form a ball out of each piece. Roll the dough pieces into circles, creating an indent in each one. Place a round of dough into the oil and fry each side for one to two minutes or until golden. Remove the dough to a paper towel so that it can drain. Repeat the process with each round. To make this bread into a sweet treat, you can sprinkle it with powdered sugar and cinnamon when it comes out.

Matzah

Matzah is a type of flatbread that Jewish people commonly have during Passover; thus, it is a culturally significant bread to many people. It resembles a cracker and can be made at home without much fuss. All you need is five simple ingredients to bring this recipe to life. There are special rules that Jews will have to follow to make this bread for Passover.

Ingredients:

- 1 cup flour
- 1 teaspoon olive oil
- .66 cup water

- .5 teaspoon kosher salt
- 1 teaspoon flour for dusting

Instructions:

Begin by preheating the oven to 475 degrees. Move the oven rack so that it is near the top of the oven. Place a baking sheet in the oven to heat it with the oven. Mix the ingredients until they become a ball and knead intensely for around one minute. Divide your dough into four pieces and then cut each piece in half again so that you have eight pieces. Roll these balls into five-inch discs and then roll them until they are eight inches. Let the dough sit for several minutes before giving a final roll so that the dough is very thin—Pierce twenty-five holes in each piece of bread to avoid it rising. Flip the pieces and repeat the piercing process. Take the sheet from the oven, and put the rounds onto the sheet; put the sheet back into the oven, and heat for two minutes. Turn over the bread and then heat for another two minutes until the bread is browned. Brush each one with olive oil and add salt. To be fit for Passover, you must use Passover flour, and from the time you add the bread and water, you only have eighteen minutes to complete the baking process.

CHAPTER 7: BUNS, ROLLS, AND BISCUITS

Buns and Rolls

Hamburger/ Hot Dog Buns

Imagine the fresh hamburger and hotdog buns that you can make with this recipe. These are perfect for a picnic or just an ordinary day of grilling in the summer, and they are super versatile. They will taste a bit different than the processed buns that you are used to, but they are well worth the effort, and you can make both kinds of buns with one dough, which is much easier and more affordable than having to, but two different types for picnics.

Ingredients

- 1 beaten egg with 1 tablespoon of cold water (a wash to brush on buns)
- .5 cup warm water
- 2 tablespoons sugar
- 6 to 7 cups of flour
- 2 cups warm milk

- 2 tablespoons oil
- Coarse salt (optional)
- 2 teaspoons salt
- 5 teaspoons yeast
- Caraway, sesame, or poppy seeds (optional)

Instructions:

Proof the yeast in warm water for five minutes before adding the milk, salt, oil, and half of the flour (start with 3 cups). Beat this mix so that it is very well mixed. Then, add the remaining flour until the dough shapes itself into a ball and doesn't cling to the bowl. Once the dough is a good texture, knead until you get an elastic dough that looks smooth. A bowl scraper can be particularly helpful for this dough because of its texture. Place the dough into a greased bowl and coat the dough with oil. Let the dough rise for an hour. Place the dough on a greased workspace and split into eighteen parts by dividing your dough into thirds, halving the thirds, and thirding those halves.

Then, shape the dough as you see fit, using the notes below. Place them on a greased baking sheet so that they are half an inch apart. If you want a crispier bun, place them further apart. Let the buns rise a second time for around forty-five minutes or until doubled. Preheat your oven to 400 degrees. Use an egg wash to brush the tops of the buns. You can add seeds or salt as desired.

You will bake for twenty minutes or until they reach a temperature of 190 degrees (they'll look golden). Let them cool on a wire cooling rack to ensure their crusts are maintained.

Special Notes

To make hamburgers: form into a round shape that's a bit smaller than the hamburger you will be serving. Generally, you'll want to make them around three and a half inches in diameter.

To make hotdogs: you can buy specialty hotdog bun pans or shape them to be cylindrical around the size of your hotdogs (aim for them to be around four and a half inches long)! You'll want to flatten the dough slightly a bit so that you get a rounded top after they rise.

Slow Buns

These slow buns are a sweet treat that will make you want more. They are traditionally started in the evening and then are baked in the morning after a long rise. This recipe comes from my mother, whose instructions are sparse because of how many times she's made this recipe. I've dressed them up a bit for your convenience and to add some clarity to this classic recipe. With a whopping six cups of flour, this recipe will make a large amount (and you'll need a big mixing bowl). These are great for making sticky buns or just to eat as a slightly sweet roll. In time, you may know this recipe by heart just as my mother does, and I do too.

Ingredients:

- .5 cup sugar
- .5 cup oil
- 6 cups flour
- 1 teaspoon of yeast
- 1 teaspoon salt
- 1 egg, beaten
- 1.5 cups warm water

Instructions:

Begin at six in the evening the day before you want to make these buns. Proof the yeast using the water and the sugar. Add the egg, salt, and oil to the proofed mix. Then, gradually incorporate the flour. Let the dough rise. At eight in the evening, punch the dough down. At ten in the evening, shape and place your dough into greased pans. Cover the dough and let the buns rise until the morning. In the morning, preheat the oven to 350 degrees and let the buns bake for twenty minutes. When you take these out of the oven, you can brush them with butter if you desire.

Parker House Rolls

This recipe is a quintessential roll recipe that never fails to impress. These rolls are ideal for holiday celebrations and everyday meals alike, and no bread cookbook would be complete without them! This recipe will make around twenty-five rolls, which is good because you'll probably want to eat at least two!

Ingredients:

- .5 cup butter
- .5 cup sugar
- 3 large eggs, beaten
- .5 cup butter for brushing
- .5 cup warm water
- 1.5 cups milk

- 2.5 teaspoons yeast
- 6 cups flour
- 1 teaspoon salt

Instructions:

Start by warming the milk in a pan until it is brought to a simmer. Take the pan off the heat and then add your butter and sugar. Allow this mixture to cool for several minutes. While it cools, proof the yeast in the warm water until it gets sudsy, about five minutes. Combine the milk mix with the eggs, salt, and yeast. Add ½ of the flour. Mix until the dough is slick. Add the rest of the flour gradually, and mix until a ball forms. Knead for five minutes before placing in a greased bowl and letting it rise to double its size, which takes an hour usually. Punch down the dough before shaping the rolls. Let the shaped rolls sit for an extra half-hour. For twenty minutes, bake at 350 degrees. When they are golden, take the rolls from the oven, and with melted butter, brush their tops to maintain a soft exterior.

Orange Rolls

With a nice orange flavor, these orange rolls only require one rise, so you can get them done in no time! This is a recipe perfect for absolute beginners because it uses a hot roll mix that you can buy at stores!

Ingredients:

- .25 cup warm water
- 2 teaspoons orange concentrate
- 1 package hot roll mix (or 3 cups of the homemade version) + 2 ½ teaspoons yeast
- .75 cup sour cream
- 1 egg
- 2 teaspoons baking powder

For Hot Roll Mix:

- .75 cup instant nonfat powdered milk
- .75 cup sugar
- 1 tablespoon salt
- 10 cups all-purpose flour

Instructions:

For hot roll mix:

Combine all ingredients thoroughly. That's all you have to do to create your own hot roll mix, which is much cheaper than a store-bought mix.

For buns:

Dissolve the yeast in water. You can then mix in the rest of the ingredients, slowly incorporating the hot roll mix last. Mix well, then knead the dough for five minutes. Roll the dough out and shape; however, you desire. Let the rolls rise for around an hour. At 350 degrees, bake the rolls for thirty to thirty-five minutes.

Lovely Tomato Rolls

These dainty rolls are delectable, and the tomato adds a little something special to this recipe. If you're feeling adventurous, give these rolls a try! This recipe will make a lot of rolls!

Ingredients:

- 1 cup lard
- 1 tablespoon salt
- 2.5 teaspoons yeast
- .5 cup sugar
- 2 cups warm tomato juice
- 2 eggs
- 8 cups flour

Instructions:

Sift the flour and then measure it out and sift it again with the salt. Proof the yeast in a small portion of the tomato juice and half the sugar. Cream the lard with the rest of the sugar and add the eggs to the yeast mix. Then, alternate between adding the dry ingredients and the creamed sugar mix to the yeast mix. Allow your dough rise for one hour and then store in the fridge until you are ready to cook it. When ready to shape, knead, and form into the shape you want. I suggest a greased muffin pan. Let the dough double in size before baking for around fifteen minutes at 425 degrees.

Rich Rolls

Ingredients:

- .5 cup scaled milk
- 6 cups flour
- 1 cup sugar
- 1 teaspoon salt
- 2.5 teaspoons yeast
- 4 eggs, beaten
- 1 cup shortening

Instructions:

Mix the scalded milk with the sugar. After it is lukewarm, add the yeast and let it sit until foamy. Mix in half the flour, and you should mix your dough well. Allow the dough rest until it doubles in size, which takes around an hour. Add the salt, eggs, shortening, and the rest of the flour. Let the dough double again. Punch the dough down. Chill for an hour at least, but this dough can remain in the fridge for several days. Shape and for twenty-five to thirty minutes bake at 350 degrees.

Fridge Rolls

These rolls will need to cool in the fried before you get them out and bake them, but they will taste great and be perfect for family meals.

Ingredients:

- .5 cup sugar
- 2 eggs, beaten
- 1 teaspoon salt
- .5 cup warm water
- 1 cup mashed potatoes
- 1 cup scaled milk
- 2.5 teaspoons yeast

- 5 to 6 cups flour
- .66 cup shortening

Instructions:

In water, dissolve the yeast. For five minutes, let the yeast sit in the water so that it foams. Add the shortening, mashed potatoes, sugar, and the salt to the yeast. Mix and then add the eggs. Add your flour until your dough is stiff. When the mixed, knead the dough for ten minutes. Let the dough rise slightly in the fridge (not doubled), which will take around an hour. Shape the dough into tolls and let the rolls rise until they become airy—Bake at 375 degrees for around twenty minutes.

Biscuits

Biscuits, at least in North America, are a type of bread that tends to be crumblier and use shortening to give them a melt in your mouth flavor. They are a quick bread, which are similar to scones but have no or not as much sugar. Biscuits often, but not always, using baking soda as a leavening agent rather than yeast. They are a known staple of the American South, but they are seen across the country and beyond.

Stir and Roll Biscuits

These biscuits will hit the spot, and they come in regular and buttermilk varieties, so you can try both to see which one you like best (they're both excellent, but I prefer buttermilk). I guarantee that they both taste great. This recipe makes about sixteen biscuits. It won't take you too long to devour these delightful biscuits. With how easy they are to make, it won't be long before you're already making your second batch!

Ingredients:

Regular:

- 3 teaspoon baking powder
- 2 cups flour
- 1 teaspoon salt
- .33 cup oil
- .66 cup milk

Buttermilk:

- 2 cups flour
- .25 teaspoon baking soda
- 1 teaspoon salt
- 2 teaspoon baking powder
- .33 cup oil
- .66 cup buttermilk

Instructions:

Begin by preheating the oven to 450 degrees. Then, as the oven preheats, you should put the baking soda, baking powder, salt, and flour into a bowl until they are thoroughly combined. Once they have been combined, you should pour the milk and oil into a measuring cup and stir in this mix with the dry goods. Stir the mixture until the ingredients form a ball that doesn't stick to the side of the bowl. Once it has been mixed, you can knead the dough. Put the dough onto a sheet of wax paper and fold it in, kneading until the dough is stretchy. When it is kneaded, you can roll the dough until it is half an inch thick and put in an ungreased pan to bake for ten to twelve minutes. They'll be done when they start to get golden on the top. You can then pull them out of the oven and enjoy these fantastic biscuits.

Cheese Biscuits

These are classic biscuits with a cheesy twist. They are great for eating at a tea time or when you want to provide lighter fare and stick to finger foods. They are best when served warm, but they will taste good for a few days after you make them. This recipe will make around twelve biscuits, but it's easy to double if you need more. The cheese in these biscuits make them more filling, and even more delicious.

Ingredients:

- ½ teaspoon dry mustard
- ¾ cup grated mild cheddar cheese (or another cheese of your choice)
- ½ teaspoon salt
- 1 egg, beaten
- 2 ½ teaspoons baking powder
- 2 cups flour
- 2/3 cup milk
- 4 tablespoons cold butter, cut into ½ inch cubes

Instructions:

Preheat your oven to 450 degrees. Sift the dry ingredients into a large bowl and then add the butter, mixing into the dry ingredients until you get a crumble with pea-sized clumps. Add ½ cup of the cheese. Create an opening in the center of the ingredients. When your hole has been made, add the milk and egg gently. Roll out the dough and either cut into triangles or squares. Brush biscuits with milk and sprinkle with the rest of the cheese. Allow the biscuits to sit for fifteen minutes and then bake for fifteen minutes.

Angel Biscuits

These biscuits taste heavenly as if angels delivered them. I found this recipe in an old church cookbook, and with some tweaks of my own, I've taken these biscuits to the next level. They've become my go-to biscuit. I love how this recipe combines the leavening power of baking soda, baking powder, and yeast.

Ingredients:

- .5 cup warm water
- 1 teaspoon baking soda
- .75 cup shortening
- 2 cups buttermilk
- 2 teaspoons baking powder
- 1 teaspoon salt
- 2.5 teaspoons yeast
- 5 cups flour

Instructions:

Dissolve your yeast in water. Add the baking soda, honey, salt, and baking powder. Then, add the shortening and the buttermilk. Gradually incorporate the flour. You can then either drop the dough onto your pan or roll it out before placing it on an oil cookie pan. At 400 degrees, bake this recipe for twelve minutes.

Baking Powder Biscuits

This is one of the simplest biscuit recipes that you'll ever find. You'll have them ready to eat in less than an hour, and you can make them with ingredients that you probably already have in your house.

Ingredients:

- 1 cup milk
- 3 teaspoons baking powder
- 1 teaspoon salt
- 2 cups flour
- .25 cup shortening

Instructions:

Mix the ingredients togher. Allow your dough to sit for fifteen minutes before rolling it out. Put these biscuits on a greased sheet and bake in a 400-degree oven for twelve minutes.

Supreme Biscuits

These biscuits are a classic biscuit, but they have an especially crumbly and rich texture, which is why they are so supreme.

Ingredients:

- .5 cup shortening
- 4 teaspoons baking powder
- .5 teaspoon salt
- 2 teaspoons sugar
- .66 cup milk
- .5 teaspoon cream of tartar
- 2 cups sifted flour

Instructions:

Mix the dry ingredients. Cut the shortening into the dry ingredients until you get pea-sized chunks; add the milk. Knead the dough for ten minutes before rolling it out so that it is one-half-inch thick. Cut the dough into your desired shape and then bake at 450 degrees for around ten to twelve minutes. If you place biscuits close to each other in the pan, they will rise higher.

CHAPTER 8: SNACKS, SWEETS, AND PARTY BREADS

Bread can be a great addition to parties, be sweetened, and also be a snack, further showing how versatile bread is! The bread in this section will perhaps be the most fun bread in the whole book and will have unique flavors that you may not normally associate with bread. These ideas will give you more to fo than merely classic loaves of bread, and some of these may be hard to find in stores, meaning you'll be creating something that can't be purchased! Even if you can buy it, it won't taste nearly as good as the bread you make yourself (of course).

Snacks

These foods are great for a snack or as appetizers. These recipes will make you feel happy and fulfill any snacky urges that you may have. Kids will love them, and you will too! Many of these won't take too much of your time, and these snacks will be healthier and taste better than store-bought counterparts, so feel free to indulge just a little!

Quick Pretzels

Pretzels couldn't be made easier with this recipe. You'll never want to buy a soft pretzel again once you realize how easy making them at home is. If you want a fast pretzel recipe, this is the one for you. You won't need to sit around waiting for the dough to rise, and the crust of the pretzel will be nice and soft and just chewy enough. You can use the flour of your choosing, but bread flour will use extra well. If you've got thirty-minutes, you have sufficient time for this pretzel. They're great with cinnamon, chocolate, or other dips.

Ingredients:

- 1 tablespoon sugar
- 1 beaten egg
- 1 teaspoon salt
- 2.5 teaspoons yeast
- 4 cups flour
- Coarse sea salt, to sprinkle on top
- 1.5 cups warm water

Instructions:

Begin by preheating the oven to 425 degrees. Spray your sheets lightly with cooking spray or brush melted butter onto them. Proof your yeast in the water, stirring for about a minute. It's okay if there are a few clumps of yeast that remain. Next, add salt and sugar and combine them with the yeast mix. Gradually add three cups of flour and combine until your mix becomes thick. Add the remaining flour until the dough isn't sticky, and you can poke it with your finger. Knead the dough surface for approximately three minutes. Then, once it is elastic, cut the dough into sections that are whatever size you want your pretzels to be. Roll the pretzel pieces into ropes, depending on how big your pretzels are. Bring the ends of the rope so that they meet and fold them into the pretzel shape. If you want, you can stick to just pretzel rods.

The next step is optional, but it helps the pretzels bake better. You can boil a pot of water with baking soda and dip the pretzels into the water for twenty to thirty seconds. When it is ready to be removed from the water, the pretzel should float. Place the pretzels on a cloth to let them dry a bit. Then, put the pretzels on your baking sheet.

Beat your egg in a small dish and place it into a shallow pan or dish. Dunk your pretzels into the egg wash so that they are submerged and covered on all sides. Put your pretzels back on the pan and sprinkle with salt (or herbs if you'd like to go that route). Bake the pretzels for ten minutes at the preheated temperature and then switch to broiling them in your oven to brown them for five minutes more. Serve with dips or sprinkled on toppings of your choice.

Extra Rich Pretzels

These pretzels take just a bit more time, but they are extra decadent and taste undeniably wonderful. As my favorite soft pretzel recipe, I cannot recommend these enough. You'll feel like you've gone to the fair or picked up a pretzel at a cart in the mall. Hot pretzels don't have to be reserved for special occasions anymore! Be careful. This recipe can be addictive. Like the easier pretzels before this one, these pretzels are great when sprinkled with cinnamon and sugar, chocolate, dipped in cheese or mustard. I love drizzling them in caramel. They're also good with just a little salt sprinkled on.

Ingredients:

- .25 cup kosher salt (for on top)
- 1 teaspoon sugar
- 1 egg (for egg wash)
- .5 cup baking soda
- .5 cup sugar
- 1.25 cups warm water
- 1.5 teaspoons salt
- 1 tablespoon vegetable oil
- 4 cups hot water
- 4 teaspoons yeast
- 5 cups flour

Instructions:

Dissolve the yeast with the sugar and the 1 ¼ warm water; let this mix rest for ten minutes. Mix the flour, salt, and a ½ cup sugar. Create a space in the center of the bowl and combine the oil and the mix of yeast. Add more water if the mixture is too dry. Knead for about seven minutes. When the dough is smooth, put the dough in a lightly oiled bowl and coat the dough with the oil. Cover the dough, and let it sit for around an hour so that the dough doubles.

Start by preheating your oven to 450 degrees. Additionally, ready two greased cookie sheets. You can use parchment or a baking mat. In a new bowl, dissolve baking soda in the 4 cups of boiling water. As that dissolves, put the dough on a floured workspace and split your dough into twelve equal pieces (or more if you want smaller pretzels). Make a rope from each piece of dough and shape it however you'd like. Put each pretzel in your hot water mix and then put them on your baking tray. If you'd like, beat an egg and brush the tops of pretzels with your egg wash. With salt, garnish your pretzels and then bake them in the oven for around eight minutes. Serve with topping of your choice. Chocolate or caramel both taste irresistible with the saltiness of these pretzels, but alternatively, I like to sprinkle them with rosemary for a more gourmet touch.

Homemade Crackers

Maybe you've never thought about making crackers at home, but homemade crackers are perfect because you can control what's in them to ensure that you are eating exactly what you like without dangerous fats such as trans fats that can sometimes be in store crackers. You'll be surprised by how manageable this recipe is. All you need are five ingredients! You can customize these crackers to include seeds that you prefer as well as herbs, so the possibilities are endless, and everyone will enjoy some version of this delightful snack.

Ingredients:

- 1 cup water
- 4 tablespoons olive oil (or other oil of your choice)
- 3 cups flour
- 2 teaspoons salt
- 2 teaspoons sugar

Add ons:

- 1 tablespoon seas salt, sesame seeds, fennel seeds, poppy seeds, or herbs. These can be sprinkled on top.

Instructions:

Start by preheating the oven to 450 degrees. Make sure your oven rack is towards the bottom of your oven. Sprinkle your baking sheet with just a bit of flour before putting it off to the side. Stir together your dry ingredients in a mid-sized bowl. Then, mix in the oil and water until you create a soft, slightly sticky dough. Ensure that no loose flour remains. Add additional water if there is excess flour. Split the dough and start with one half of the dough. Make your dough into a square and roll it out to, at a maximum, a 1/8-inch thickness. Add toppings if desired by brushing the dough with water and sprinkling the toppings on. Cut the dough into the desired size and put your crackers on your baking tray. They can be placed close together. Pierce the crackers with a fork. Bake your crackers for twelve to fifteen minutes or until the edges start to turn golden.

After the first batch, repeat the process with your second half of dough. These crackers should be cooled on wire racks and stored in an airtight container. They last around five days, which shouldn't be a problem given how quickly you'll want to devour these.

Sweets

If you've got a sweet tooth, these recipes will be for you! Bread doesn't just have to be savory. Some of my favorite recipes have a sweetness to them! These breads will be ideal for dessert or even just as a midday snack. Or, if you're like my dad, you can have them for breakfast!

Classic Doughnuts

Doughnuts are often associated with breakfast, but eat them at every chance I get. This recipe will give you an easy method of making glazed doughnuts. These doughnuts aren't the healthiest option, but if you're going to treat yourself, why not go all out? One doughnut once in a while won't hurt you. In fact, I think these doughnuts might improve your life.

Ingredients:

For the dough:

- .5 teaspoon vanilla extract
- 1 teaspoon sugar
- .25 cup sugar
- 6 tablespoons melted butter
- 2.5 teaspoons yeast
- 2 eggs
- 1 cup whole milk

- 4.5 cups flour
- .5 teaspoon Kosher salt
- Oil, for frying

For the glaze:

- ¼ cup whole milk
- ½ teaspoon vanilla extract
- 2 cup powdered sugar

Instructions:

Begin by greasing a large bowl. Then, heat the milk for forty seconds in the microwave or on the stove. Proof the yeast in the milk with the teaspoon of sugar. Wait until it is foamy, which should take less than ten minutes. Whisk together in a separate bowl, your flour, and salt. Then, add the rest of the sugar, the eggs, the butter, and the vanilla. Incorporate the yeast mixture and the dry ingredients. Stir until the dough becomes shaggy. Next, knead the dough until it becomes stretchy. Add more flour if you need to. Place the dough in your greased bowl and let it rise for an hour until it has doubled. Roll your dough into a rectangle that is half an inch thick. Cut out your doughnuts with a doughnut cutter. Place the doughnuts on your baking tray and let them rise for forty minutes longer.

As they rise, make your glaze. Simply mix all your ingredients, and then put the mix aside.

Using a Dutch oven or a heavy pot, heat around two inches of oil until the oil is 350 degrees. Cook the doughnuts in the oil in batches for about one minute per side. If you're cooking doughnut holes, use less time for cooking. Take doughnuts out of oil when they are a dark golden color and put them on a tray lined with paper towels. Let them cool for a few minutes before drizzling them with the glaze. You can cool them on a rack or eat them without delay.

Delicious Sweet Bread

This sweet bread is a great recipe that can be served as its own entity or made into sticky buns. Whatever you choose to do with them, they will be a hit with whoever you serve them to. These are wonderful with a warm cup of cocoa on a cold evening.

Ingredients:

- .5 cup mashed potatoes
- 2 eggs, beaten
- .5 cup warm water
- 1.75 cup milk
- 1 teaspoon baking powder
- 1 teaspoon salt
- .5 cup shortening
- 1 teaspoon vanilla
- 2.5 teaspoons yeast
- .5 cup sugar
- 6 cups flour

Instructions :

Begin by scalding your milk. Then add the sugar and mashed potatoes. Let this mixture cool. Add the yeast to the warm water so it can dissolve for five minutes. Incorporate the yeast with the milk mixture. Then stir in the eggs and the vanilla; add the baking powder and salt to the milk. Add the flour gradually. Knead for ten minutes. Let the dough rise until it doubles, which will take up to an hour and a half. Punch the dough down before shaping. In greased plans, place the rolled-out buns. Allow the dough to rise again before baking at 350 degrees for forty-five minutes.

Cinnamon Rolls

Many bakers, myself included, don't need a recipe for cinnamon rolls because, primarily, all you have to do is roll out any kind of bread dough you want and fill that dough with sugar and cinnamon. Much of this practice can be guestimated, but for people with less experience, it can help to have a dedicated cinnamon roll recipe.

My grandmother, when she made her bread each week, would take what was left of her bread dough from her regular loaves and make cinnamon rolls out of that dough. She'd roll it out and fill it before adding a cinnamon mixture to drizzle on top and sticking these gooey treats in the oven. While you can use practically any bread dough you want, I will provide a dough that I love you use for cinnamon rolls to get you on track.

Once you've made these cinnamon rolls, you'll never prefer the ones that you find in the mall again! I've included an icing recipe, but if there's a recipe that you favor, feel free to use that instead.

Ingredients:

For the dough:

- .5 cup sugar
- 1 teaspoon salt
- 4.5 cups flour

- .33 cup melted butter that has cooled slightly
- 2.5 teaspoons yeast
- 2 eggs
- 1 cup warm milk

For the filling:

- .25 cup white sugar
- .5 cup heavy cream (which you will pour over rolls when they have risen)
- 1 stick butter
- 1 cup brown sugar

For the icing:

- .5 tablespoon maple extract or vanilla extract
- .33 cup butter softened
- 2.5 cups powdered sugar
- 8 ounces cream cheese, softened

Instructions:

Proof the yeast in the warm milk. Mix in the eggs, salt, sugar, and butter. Add four cups of flour and then add the additional ½ cup as needed. Mix until just barely mixed and then let the mix rest for several minutes. Your flour should absorb the liquids. Beat the dough, so it is more mixed and then knead it for five minutes until it is tacky and sticks to the side of the bowl slightly.

Place the dough into a greased bowl and then let it rise until it has doubled, which will take around thirty minutes.

As the dough rises, combine the butter, sugar, and cinnamon until they are well mixed. Once the dough has risen, roll it out so that it is thin. With a knife or spatula, spread the filling over the surface of the dough. Then, tightly roll the dough. From there, you can cut the roll with a knife and place the slices into a baking pan. Let the dough rest for twenty minutes. Preheat the oven to 375 degrees and heat the heavy cream so that it is warm but not hot. Pour the warm cream over the risen rolls— Bake for twenty to twenty-two minutes. The cooking times will vary based on the size of the rolls and the pan you are using, so watch them carefully. You want them to be golden.

As the rolls cool, you can begin to make the icing. Combine the butter and the cream cheese and mix them well. Then, add the powdered sugar and extract. Once the rolls have cooled, you can spread the icing and serve your delightful dessert.

Party Bread

Party bread is a type of bread that is perfect for bringing to a party and is stuffed with foods that aren't just the bread itself, such as meat, cheese, or herbs. This type of bread is full of flavor and is sure to impress any of your friends or your family. Party breads can be great if you're looking to make an offbeat dinner that defies the same old dishes that you normally make.

Cream Cheese Bread Roll

This smooth, creamy bread roll will delight you when you try it. It is a sweeter bread and has an excellent cream cheese filling. It is an overnight bread, but you could also make it in the morning and bake it in the evening.

Ingredients:

For the dough:

- .5 cup warm water
- 1 cup sour cream
- .5 cup melted butter
- 1 teaspoon salt
- 2 eggs, beaten
- 4 cups flour
- 5 teaspoons yeast

- .5 cup sugar

For the filling:

- ¾ cup sugar
- 1/8 teaspoon salt
- 16 ounces cream cheese
- 1 beaten egg
- 2 teaspoons vanilla

Instructions:

Warm the sour cream at a low temperature so that it gets warm but doesn't boil. Add the sugar, salt, and butter. Let the mixture cool so that it is lukewarm. Place the yeast in the water and wait until it bubbles. Then add this yeast mixture to the sour cream mixture, add the eggs, and then slowly incorporate the flour. Cover and refrigerate overnight. Roll out the dough and then cut into either four pieces or eight pieces. You'll want the dough to be thin. Mix the ingredients for the filling. Spread the cream over the pieces of dough and then roll the dough and pinch the ends. Put them on a cookie sheet and ensure the pieces have room. Let the bread rest for one hour, but do not expect it to rise much. Bake the dough at 375 degrees for fifteen minutes; slit two-inch slits down the loaf for ventilation. Put powdered sugar on top.

Casserole Dill Bread

This is an offbeat bread that is packed with ingredients that you might not expect to find in bread. Nevertheless, it is an excellent addition to any breadmaker's repertoire. This heavy dough will make a fantastic loaf and is quite satiating. It has a unique ingredient: potato soup.

Ingredients

- 1 can condensed potato soup
- 1 tablespoon instant onion
- 2 tablespoons shortening
- 2 teaspoons dillweed
- 1 egg
- 5 teaspoons yeast
- .66 cup water
- 3 tablespoons sugar
- 4.5 cups flour
- 1 teaspoon salt

Instructions:

Mix two cups of the flour with the sugar, yeast, and salt. In a separate pan, add the soup and smash the potato lumps with a fork. Add the water, onion, your shortening. Heat until the mix is warm. Add to the yeast mixture. Add the egg, dill, and the rest of the flour; mix for two minutes. Cover the dough and let it rest for one hour so that it doubles. Keep in mind that this dough should be heavy and sticky. Knead for three minutes. Then, spoon into a baking dish. Let it double in size again. Bake at 375 degrees for forty-five minutes or until it has browned. You can brush the top with additional shortening if you wish. Cut and serve in wedges.

Ingredients

Whole Grain Cheese Herb Bread

If you're looking for a party bread that is also whole grain, this bread is an excellent choice. With cheese and herbs filling this bread, you can't go wrong. It tastes decadent without having *too much* stuff in it, but the list of ingredients is, admittedly, longer than it is for most types of bread. Regardless, it's worth the fuss. This recipe will make one small load.

Ingredients

- .5 teaspoon baking soda
- .5 teaspoon basil
- 1 tablespoon vegetable oil
- .5 teaspoon salt
- .5 teaspoons parsley
- 2 tablespoons grated parmesan
- .75 cup water
- 2 tablespoons vital gluten (optional)
- 1 teaspoon yeast
- .66 cup grated cheese (cheddar or swiss)
- 2.25 cup whole wheat flour
- 2 tablespoons fruit juice concentrate
- 2 teaspoons maple sugar

Instructions:

Begin by proofing the yeast in the water, maple sugar, and fruit juice concentrate. Wait five minutes. Add the vital gluten if you're using it. Then add the oil. Mix in the salt, baking soda, basil, and parsley. Next, add the grated cheese and parmesan. Finally, mix in the flour until you get a dough ball. Knead five minutes and then let it rest for forty-five minutes or until it has doubled. Shape the dough into whatever kind of loaf that you'd want. Let it rest for another half an hour—Bake at 425 degrees for twenty to twenty-five minutes.

Italian Party Bread

This bread is sure to please with all the meat and cheese that is packed inside of it. If you're not feeling Italian, you can swap out the meat and cheese for some from other cultures. For example, to make it French, you can use Gruyere cheese, or for a Spanish version, you can use Serrano ham and Manchego cheese. The possibilities are endless. This is a great recipe to apply a little bit of creative genius. Fit this recipe to include whatever meats and cheese you love best, and you'll adore the outcome.

Ingredients:

- 1 premade <u>pizza dough</u> of your choice.
- 1 tablespoon butter (to brush on top)
- 1 tablespoon flour for dusting
- .33 cup banana peppers, diced
- .33 cup pesto sauce, prepared
- 2 ounces sliced prosciutto, cut into ribbons
- 6 slices provolone cheese
  (you can swap out whatever meats and cheese that you may prefer to customize this recipe to your liking).

Instructions:

Preheat the oven to 450 degrees. Line a pan with parchment paper or a baking mat. Roll pizza dough into a rectangle that's 1/8 inch thick; add the pesto sauce to the dough, allowing a 1-inch border around the perimeter of the dough. Top the dough with cheese, prosciutto, and banana peppers. Roll the dough up and press it down. Dust the roll with flour. Cut the dough lengthwise so that you have three strips. Braid the strips and pull the ends together so that you have a circular load. Bake for thirty minutes and let the bread cool a bit before you serve it. You can brush the warm loaf with butter if you want. You can serve it warm or serve it at room temperature.

CHAPTER 9: FLOURLESS BREAD

Some people, for whatever reason, aren't able to tolerate bread that has gluten in it. Those people will struggle to find affordable bread in stores. Gluten-free options are incredibly expensive, which can be disheartening for people who love bread but are allergic or intolerant. Fear not, there are plenty of recipes that don't require any normal flour, and you can make them pretty easily in your kitchen and save a massive amount of money. Even if you can tolerate gluten, these recipes can be fun to try if you want to cut down on how much flour you are using or merely want to experience using other grains to make bread. Most of these recipes will use premixed gluten-free flour blends and xanthan gum. Some mixes may already have xanthan gum, so if yours does, leave it out of the recipe to maintain the needed chemical balance.

Loaves

Looking to cut out gluten while still wanting to eat loaves of bread? Save yourself a bunch of money by making these breads yourself. They're all pretty easy and don't require any ingredients that are that outlandish.

Gluten-Free Sandwich Bread

You don't have to sacrifice good sandwich bread simply because you're on a gluten-free diet, or a loved one is gluten-free. This recipe will only make one loaf, but it's best eaten quickly, so it is better to make one loaf at a time if you can so that it doesn't go to waste.

Ingredients:

- 1.25 teaspoons xanthan gum
- 3 eggs
- 1 cup warm milk
- 2 teaspoons yeast
- 3 cups gluten-free flour
- 1.25 teaspoons salt
- 3 tablespoons sugar

Instructions:

Add the sugar, salt, yeast, xanthan gum, and flour in a large bowl and mix, so they are well combined. Add the milk to get rid of the crumbly texture of the dough. Next, mix in the butter and the eggs gradually. Mix until you get a heavy dough. Allow the dough to rise for one hour. Punch down the dough. Put the dough in a greased loaf pan. Let the bread rise again until it comes just over the top of the pan, which takes from forty-five minutes to one hour. Preheat the oven to 350 degrees as the bread rises. You can then bake the bread for thirty-six to forty-five minutes or until it becomes golden.

If you want, you can shape this bread into dinner rolls and make gluten-free dinner rolls.

Gluten-Free French Bread

You won't notice or care that this bread doesn't have any wheat in it! You can't go wrong with nice French bread. This is a single rise bread, which makes it easier than your average French bread. You can replace the flours provided for a preblended mix of gluten-free flour, but I enjoy the combination of tapioca flour and rice flour.

Ingredients

- 1.5 teaspoons salt
- 1 cup tapioca flour
- 2 egg whites, beaten
- 1 teaspoon vinegar
- 2 cups rice flour
- 1.5 cups warm water
- 2 tablespoons butter
- 2 tablespoons fast-rising yeast
- 2 tablespoons sugar
- 3 teaspoons xanthan gum

Instructions

Mix the various flours, salt, and xanthan gum. In another bowl, proof the yeast the water with your sugar; add the yeast with the dry ingredients. Then, incorporate the butter, vinegar, and egg whites. Mix thoroughly. Shape the dough and slash the top of your loaves diagonally. Let it rise for thirty minutes before baking in the oven at 400 degrees for forty to forty-five minutes.

Gluten-Free Italian Bread

For lovers of a nice loaf of Italian bread, here's one that's served at dinner parties where you're hosting a gluten-intolerant person. Everyone, gluten lovers and haters alike, can enjoy this bread. This bread is a fan favorite, so it's sure to please even the pickiest eaters. For that reason, t's my go-to gluten-free bread when I'm having people over.

Ingredients:

- 2 teaspoons kosher salt
- 2 cups milk
- 4 tablespoons melted butter
- 2 tablespoons sugar
- 2 teaspoons yeast
- 3 cups gluten-free bread flour

Instructions:

In a large bowl or mixer, add the flour, yeast, sugar, and salt. Slowly add the butter and the milk. Then mix some more until the ingredients are all incorporated and a ball forms. Let the dough rise for two hours until it has doubled. If you choose to refrigerate this dough, you should wait for at least four hours and can wait up to a week to use it. When the dough has doubled, put it on a floured surface and let rise as the oven preheats at 450 degrees. Put your baking stone or baking tray in the oven as it preheats. As the pan heats, roll your dough and shape it. Create stems in your oven when you put your rolled-out dough into the oven. Bake the dough for thirty to thirty-five minutes. Brush with butter when it comes out if you'd like.

Rolls and Biscuits

Yes, you can have dinner rolls and biscuits too! They'll be delicious.

Gluten-Free Dinner Rolls

These are an ideal basic dinner roll for gluten-free people, and all you have to do is use the <u>Gluten-Free Sandwich Bread</u> or the <u>Gluten-Free French Bread</u> and shape them into dinner rolls rather than dinner rolls. Cook them for less time given their small size, so start with baking them at 425 degrees for twelve to fifteen minutes and go from there. They'll be done when they are golden colored. Brush with butter when they come out so that they have a nice crust. Alternatively, you can give them an egg wash before you put them in the oven to also create a good crust.

Gluten-Free Biscuits

These melt in your mouth biscuits don't need wheat flour to take out of this world. Not only are these biscuits gluten-free, but they are also dairy-free (you can swap the dairy-free parts in for dairy if you'd like)! You may be wondering how they can missing so much and still taste so good.

Ingredients:

- .5 teaspoon salt
- .5 teaspoon xanthan gum
- 1 tablespoon gluten-free baking powder
- 1 cup "buttermilk" (use almond or cashew milk with a tablespoon of vinegar mixed in)
- 1 large egg (for a vegan dish you can use egg replacer)
- 2 cups gluten-free flour
- 2 tablespoons gluten-free flour
- 2 tablespoons sugar
- 6 tablespoons vegan butter or shortening

Instructions:

Begin by preheating your oven to 450 degrees. Then add the flour, baking powder, sugar, and salt into a bowl. Cut the butter into small pieces. You want to mix the cut butter into the dry ingredients. Incorporate it using a pastry cutter until you get pea-sized chunks. Add your milk. Then, beat the egg and add it. Your dough should be sticky but not tough. Mix the dough, but be careful not to mix it too much. You want to keep your butter chunks to maintain a flaky taste. Put a small portion of flour onto parchment paper and then add the dough, but don't roll it out. With flour, dust the biscuit tops, and then knead the dough twice. Form rough rounds that are an inch thick and have a seven-inch diameter. Then, using a jar top or a specific biscuit cutter, cut out your biscuits. Then, put your biscuits on a cookie sheet. Bake them for fifteen to twenty-five minutes and then butter them on top.

Fun Stuff

What's life without a little fun? From pizza to pretzels to cinnamon rolls, you can have it all. You'll be full, but you'll be happy!

Gluten-Free Pizza Crust

This pizza crust will appeal to pizza lovers everywhere.

Ingredients:

- .75 cup warm water
- 2 cups gluten-free flour
- 1 tablespoon sugar
- 2.5 teaspoons yeast
- 1 egg
- 1 tablespoon olive oil
- 1 teaspoon apple cider vinegar
- 1 teaspoon salt

Instructions:

Put a baking sheet in the oven as you preheat the oven to 450 degrees. As the oven preheats, combine the sugar, yeast, and water so that it can proof for five minutes. While the yeast proofs, mix the flour and salt. Then, add the yeast mix, olive oil, and egg. Mix it until the ingredients are all well mixed. Take the dough out from the bowl and spread onto your pan. Bake for eight to ten minutes and then take it out to add toppings. After the toppings are on, bake for another eight to ten minutes until the cheesy is bubbly, and the crust is golden. Wait five minutes before cutting and serving it.

Gluten-Free Soft Pretzels

Just like the pretzels you'd find in the mall but without any gluten! Like any pretzel, you can dip these in any dip that you like. I love these pretzels, especially with melted cheese! You won't know that they aren't the real thing!

Ingredients:

For the dough:

- 1.25 cup warm water
- 1.25 teaspoons salt
- .5 teaspoon baking powder
- 1 egg
- 1 teaspoon xanthan gum
- 3 tablespoons brown sugar
- 2 tablespoons butter, softened
- 2 teaspoons yeast
- 3.5 cups gluten-free flour

For the water bath:

- .25 cup baking soda
- 2 tablespoons sugar
- 4 quarts boiling water

For on top:

- Salt for on top of your pretzel (optional)

Instructions:

Add the flour, sugar, baking powder, yeast, salt, and the xanthan gum into a bowl. Once those are combined, add your butter, water, and egg. Mix these all until you have a tough dough, which will take around four minutes in a mixer. Add water if your dough doesn't have enough moisture. Knead the dough for several minutes until it is elastic. Then, store it in a greased bowl and allow the dough to rise so that it nearly doubles. Preheat your oven to 425 degrees. Place the dough on a floured workspace and split into twelve parts. Shape the pretzels how you see fit.

Put baking soda and sugar into boiling water, and when the foaminess is gone, put the pretzels each in the water for around five seconds. Take them out as soon as they float. Put the pretzels on your baking sheet and sprinkle them with a coarse salt that you like. For soft pretzels, bake for eighteen to twenty minutes. If you want pretzels with more chew, bake them for twenty-five minutes. Hard pretzels will take thirty-five minutes. The pretzels should cool around ten minutes before you eat them.

Gluten-Free Cinnamon Rolls

Cinnamony, soft, and gooey, these are the perfect dessert bread that you'll want to make repeatedly. You can use any of the breads as a basis for these rolls. Just roll the dough out and add a mix that contains some butter, cinnamon, brown sugar, and white sugar. Then, roll the dough up tightly, cut it up, and place it in your pan. Drizzle with heavy whipping cream before you put it in the oven. For more information, refer to the Cinnamon Rolls recipe earlier in this book and swap the dough out for a gluten-free one. It's as easy as that!

CHAPTER 10: BREAKFAST BREAD

While you can use most of the breads in this book for toast and turn them into breakfast breads, some specific bread types are generally eaten at breakfast time. Start your morning off right with these incredible varieties of bread, and prevent midmorning hunger by starting the day the right way. They'll keep you full and happy.

Bagels

Bagels originated in Jewish communities in Poland. They can be hand-shaped into their well-known shape. Then, they are boiled before being baked, just as many pretzels are. They've become popular around the world are often eaten in the morning, but they can be eaten at all times of day! You've surely had store-bought bagels, but prepare yourself for the unique enjoyment that homemade bagels will bring!

Basic Bagels

When you just need an everyday bagel. Dress this up by adding seeds or toppings of your choice. They're great toasted (as bagels should be). You can't go wrong with a classic.

Ingredients:

For the dough:

- 1 tablespoon brown sugar
- 4 cups flour
- 1 tablespoon yeast
- 1.33 cups warm water
- 2 teaspoons salt

For water bath:

- 1 tablespoon sugar
- 2 tablespoons brown sugar
- 2 quarts boiling water

Instructions:

Mix all the ingredients for the bagel dough together and then knead for ten minutes to fifteen minutes. When you have finished kneading, put the bread in a greased bowl and let it rise until it's puffy. It's okay if it doesn't double. This should take around an hour. Put dough on a floured surface and divide the dough into twelve pieces. If you want larger bagels, use eight pieces. Roll each piece into round balls and put them on the baking sheets to sit for thirty additional minutes. You want them to rise just a bit. Start your water bath by combining all the ingredients in a large pot. The oven should be preheated to 425 degrees. When the dough has risen, poke a hole in each bagel with your finger. The hole should be about two inches in diameter. Boil the bagels for two minutes on one side and one on the other in the water and then put them on a towel to dry slightly before putting them on their baking sheet. Once all bagels have been thrown into the bath, bake them for twenty to twenty-five minutes. Flip them over after fifteen minutes of baking. Cool the bagels on a wire rack before eating.

If you want to add toppings, bake the bagels for twenty minutes, dampen them with water, add your toppings, and put them back in the oven to bake for the rest of the time.

Whole Wheat Bagels

Bagels but with a whole wheat twist!

Ingredients:

- 1.5 cups flour
- 1.5 cups warm water
- 2 tablespoons molasses
- 1 egg, beaten (to brush on top of bagels)
- 1 pot boiling water
- 1 tablespoon sugar
- 2.5 teaspoons yeast
- 2 teaspoon baking soda
- 2 teaspoons salt
- 2 cups whole wheat flour

Instructions:

Proof the yeast. Wait five minutes until the yeast starts to become foamy. Then, add the flours, salt, and molasses. Once those are incorporated, knead the dough for five to ten minutes or until it is elastic. Let the dough double its size for around an hour and a half. When the dough has doubled, preheat the oven to 425 degrees. Punch the dough down and split the dough into ten parts. Shape these parts into balls and use your finger to create a hole in the center. Boil the water and add baking soda to it; dip the bagels into the water and boil them for a minute and a half. Take the bagels out of the water and put them onto the readied baking sheets. Brush them with the egg wash, and add toppings if you'd like—Bake for twenty minutes or until they have browned. Then, wait for ten minutes before eating or storing them.

English Muffins

English muffins are small pieces of bread that are leavened with yeast and have grooves in the middle. They are primarily eaten in Australia and the United States and originated in England. They are fairly flat, and they are commonly split in half so that they can be toasted, and then people put butter, peanut butter, or jam on them. They are also a great base for Eggs Benedict!

Basic English Muffins

These are the classic English muffins that you know and love.

Ingredients:

- 1.5 teaspoons salt
- 1.75 cups warm milk
- 2 teaspoons yeast
- 3 tablespoons softened butter
- 4.5 cups flour
- 1 egg, beaten
- Semolina to sprinkle on the pan

Instructions:

Mix all the ingredients to a mixing bowl except the semolina. This dough is softer than most, so you need to be gentle when you are mixing it. Mix it until it looks shiny and satiny, which should take around five minutes. Pull your dough into a ball and then let it rise in a covered bowl for one to two hours. It may not be double its size, but it should look puffed out. Shape the dough into flattened balls with about a three-inch diameter. Let them rise for twenty more minutes. Then they will need to be cooked for eight to fifteen minutes. Use an electric griddle or a frying pan for cooking a few muffins at once. Be sure to use cooking spray if you're not using a non-stick surface. Before you put the muffins on, sprinkle them with semolina. Let the muffins cool before eating them.

Honey Whole Wheat English Muffins

These whole-wheat English muffins are so delightful because the added honey gives them a slight extra sweetness. These are perfect with jam or honey on top of them. They'll be cooked in a skillet.

Ingredients:

- .25 cup yellow cornmeal
- 1 cup buttermilk
- 2 cups white flour
- 1 teaspoon salt
- 1 tablespoon melted butter
- 2.5 teaspoons yeast
- 3 tablespoons honey
- 1 teaspoon sugar
- Oil, for the skillet

Instructions:

Heat the buttermilk so that it is warm but not hot. Dissolve the yeast in the sugar and the buttermilk and proof them for fifteen minutes until they start to bubble or foam. Then, add the yeast mix to your large mixing bowl. Add the butter, flour, and honey and mix for two to three minutes. Scrape the bowl and then mix for seven additional minutes. Place in a bowl, and the dough needs to rise for about two hours. Roll the dough out and shape it into twelve flattened balls that are around three inches in diameter. Let the dough rise for another half an hour. Brush the muffins with oil as you heat your skillet. Cook the muffins for about five minutes per side so that they become golden.

CHAPTER 11: FRUIT AND NUT BREAD

Fruit Bread

As the name would imply, fruit bread is a bread that has fruit in it. Generally, this bread is considered quick bread, so you won't have to wait for it to rise. Though, it does often have longer baking times than that of normal bread loaves. Nevertheless, it is easy to assemble. Because of the fruit, this bread is often sweet, but it is not nearly as sweet as sweet treats like cinnamon rolls. Most will take around an hour to bake with a total time of an hour and a half. This also includes mixing.

Banana Bread

Banana bread is the classic fruit bread that everyone knows and loves. It doesn't taste much like bananas, but the bananas give it its moistness and emphasize the other flavors, making this quick loaf a hit! When talking about fruit breads, this is a staple. It's also a fantastic way to use old bananas that are past their peak ripeness. When bananas start to get old, you can freeze them until you're ready to make your banana bread. You can add 1 cup walnuts if you want to make this a banana nut bread, but this bread doesn't need the nuts to taste complete.

Ingredients:

- .25 cup buttermilk
- .5 teaspoon baking powder
- .25 cup shortening
- .75 teaspoon baking soda
- 1.5 cups sugar
- .5 teaspoon salt
- 1 cup mashed bananas
- 1 teaspoon vanilla.
- 2.25 cups flour
- 2 eggs

Instructions:

Cream the sugar, shortening, and eggs; add the banana. Sift the dry ingredients. Add the milk and then add the dry ingredients; stir in the vanilla. Make sure the batter is well mixed and then add nuts if you want them in your banana bread. Grease a pan and add the dough. Bake the bread at 325 degrees for one hour or until the bread passes the cake test (insert a toothpick, and the cake is done if it comes out clean), which you can use for all the breads in this section.

Brown Bread

This dark bread is known for being filled with raisins and having a sweet molasses taste. This fruit bread pairs well with a hot cup of coffee or hot cocoa. My kids aren't a fan of fruit bread, but they love this one. I usually have to make multiple loaves when I make this recipe, which is why you can fill four small loaf pans with the recipe as provided. Feel free to halve it if you don't want that much of it.

Ingredients:

- 1.25 tablespoons shortening
- 1 cup raisins
- 2.75 cups flour
- 1.5 teaspoons vanilla
- 1 cup sugar
- 1 egg
- 2 cup water
- 2 tablespoons molasses (preferably dark)
- 2 teaspoons baking soda

Instructions:

Bring the molasses, water, and raisins to a boil. As they boil, combine the other ingredients in a mixing bowl. Turn the heat off the raisin mix and let it cool. If you'd like, add ½ cup chopped nuts. Put the dough into number two cans (which hold 2 ½ cups) and bake for 1 hour.

Fruit and Nut Bread

Many fruit breads also have nuts in them. Here are some of my favorite fruit breads that also contain nuts. You can add nuts to most of the breads in the just fruit category, like was optional for the banana bread, but these breads intentionally incorporate the nuts for a wonderful flavor balance. You'll go nuts for these fruit loaves of bread!

Cranberry Nut Bread

With the richness of cranberries and nuts, this bread tastes delightful with a cup of tea or in the morning if you want a sweet breakfast. With a touch of orange and whatever nuts you choose, the flavors come together nicely, and the citrus helps bring out the taste of the cranberries while the cranberries balance the nuts with sweetness. The combination of ingredients will hit your taste buds exactly right!

Ingredients:

- .5 teaspoons baking soda
- 1 egg
- .75 cup cranberries, chopped
- .75 cup lard

- .75 cup nuts of your choice, chopped (I suggest pecans)
- 1 teaspoon salt
- 2 cups flour
- 1.5 teaspoons baking powder
- .75 cup liquid (juice from one orange and the rest being water)
- 3 tablespoons melted butter

Instructions:

Mix the orange juice, water, butter, and egg in a bowl. Combine the liquids and the dry ingredients. Add the lard. Then, add the nuts and cranberries once the batter is thoroughly mixed. Put the batter in a greased loaf pan at 325 degrees for one hour. If you're using a glass dish, bake at 300 degrees for an hour and fifteen minutes to preserve the texture. You can eat this bread while it is still warm or wait for it to cool. It tastes fantastic either way!

California Walnut Applesauce Loaf

The applesauce provides moisture more than taste, but the walnuts are so rich (and good for you) that you can't go wrong with this bread. Feel free to use cinnamon apple sauce to add an extra spiciness to this loaf. It already has some cinnamon in it, but I often like a little extra flavor because I love cinnamon. You can also add a glaze to the top if you'd like to add an extra little something to this bread. You can substitute the walnuts for other nuts if you'd like, but if you do that, you'll have to change the name of the bread to California Nut Applesauce Loaf!

Ingredients:

- .25 teaspoon cloves
- 1.25 cup packed brown sugar
- .5 cup shortening
- .5 teaspoon nutmeg
- .75 cup chopped walnuts
- .5 teaspoon cinnamon
- 1 cup unsweetened apple sauce
- .5 teaspoon salt
- .75 teaspoon baking soda
- 1 teaspoon baking powder
- 2 cups sifted flour

Instructions:

Beat the shortening, sugar, eggs together. Add the applesauce. Sift the baking powder, soda, flour, salt, and spices before adding them to the mixing bowl. When the batter is mixed, add the nuts. At 350 degrees, bake for an hour to an hour and ten minutes. Let the bread cool or serve it warm. If you want, top with a glaze with 2 tablespoons milk, and 1 tablespoon powdered sugar, and 1 tablespoon brown sugar for an extra touch of sweetness.

Date and Nut Bread

This date and nut bread is so tasty, and the combinations of nuts and dates make this bread a perfect treat. Most people underestimate how good dates are, but they are one of the best fruits for putting into quick breads. My husband is the biggest supporter of this bread in my family, but I'm pretty into it as well.

Ingredients:

- 1.75 cups sugar
- 3.75 cups flour
- 1 tablespoon butter
- 1 cup dates, cut into small pieces
- 1 cups walnuts, chopped
- 1 egg
- 1.5 cups boiling water
- 1 teaspoon vanilla extract
- 2 teaspoons baking soda

Instructions:

Douse the dates in the boiling water and wait until the date mix cools—cream the butter and the sugar. Next, add the egg and walnuts, then the date and water combo. Add dry ingredients and then the vanilla. Place the mixture into two greased bread pans. At 350 degrees, bake your loaves for around an hour.

CHAPTER 12: PRESENT YOUR BREAD

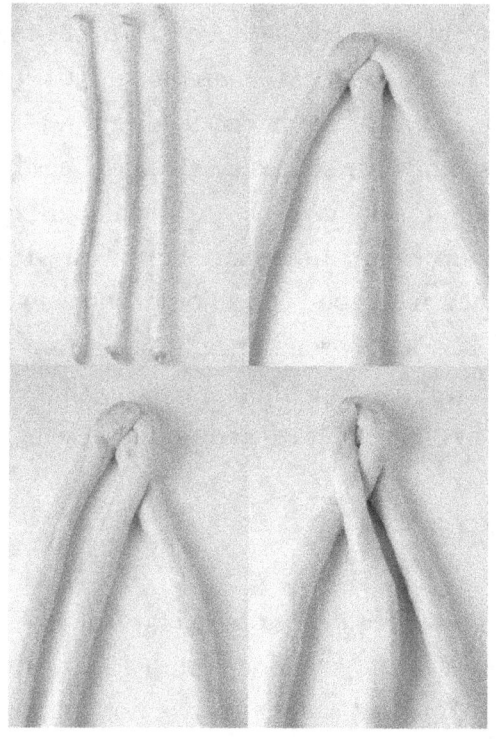

Presentation is an important part of breadmaking. You want to be able to have bread that looks good as much as it tastes good. Further, you want to be able to preserve leftovers as best as you can so that they stay as fresh as possible. Use the following tips to be sure your presentation points are top-notch.

Shaping Your Bread

For most loaves, you can be creative with how you shape your bread. That's a huge part of the fun. When you shape your loaves, you become an artist and can make your bread breathtakingly beautiful. Here are some of my favorite shapes that you can easily accomplish, even if you have no breadmaking experience. These are far from all the shapes that you will encounter, but they are a good collection of some good starter shapes. There's no wrong or right way to shape bread. Some bread types and cultures tend to shape bread in certain ways, but don't let tradition limit you.

Basic Loaf

The basic loaf requires no specialty shaping. All you have to do is push your dough into a loaf pan or form it into a cylindrical shape. There's nothing fancy here, but if you're in a rush or just want a normal loaf of bread, you can't go wrong with this once, but I do urge you to try more adventurous shapes every so often. For some breads, you may want to shape into a round loaf rather than in oblong ones; sourdough, for example, is often round.

Coils

Coils are a round bread shape that can work for small loaves or bigger loaves. To accomplish a coil, all you have to do is split your dough into 8 or 12 uniform pieces. From there, you will make ropes of your pieces. Then, you coil the ropes around each other, tucking the ends of each piece underneath the loaf. This loaf takes some patience, but it looks great once you've got it shaped and get the hang of the process. Try this one with sourdough rather than the traditional round shape. Or you can try this shape with a loaf of sweet bread. Again, don't limit yourself based on what breadmaking traditions tell you that you should do. You get to be creative during this process, so don't squander your creativity.

Bloomer

The bloomer is a simple loaf shape to make. All you have to do is shape the bread into a cylinder and create diagonal slashes on the top of the bread. This is normally found on British bread, but you can utilize it on non-British loaves as well. This style adds a little decoration to an otherwise plain loaf of bread without adding too much fuss.

Braid

For anyone who has ever tried braiding hair, this one should be pretty easy. All you have to do is divide your dough into three and create three equally sized ropes. Then, you braid, putting strand over strand until the whole loaf is braided. While most people will start at one end and work to the other, for some, it may be easier to start in the middle of the loaf and work your way out. At each end of the loaf, tuck the end pieces under so they are on the bottom of the bread. Then, you can place your bread on the baking sheet and wait for it to rise.

Mock Braid

The mock braid is a good alternative to the braid that many people will find to be less of a hassle. To make the mock braid, roll out your dough and form it into a rectangle. Cut one-inch strips down the bread on each side while leaving about one-third of the dough in the center uncut. When you have your strips cut, alternate folding one piece in from each side at an angle that's pointed towards yourself. Do this all the way down the loaf and fold in the ends of the pieces to make the loaf resemble a braid.

The Twist

This is completed exactly like the braid except instead of braiding; you twist two pieces of rope together. This is another basic method that has good-looking results that will look more impressive than they are. Whereas a braid looks more traditional, the twist can add a nice, fresh touch to your bread.

The Mock Twist

The twist is perhaps my favorite to create because of how nice it looks and how easy it is to make. My mom is partial to this shape as well. The mock twist is done just as the mock braid is except you bring the folds into the center of the bread. You will pull them to the back of the loaf and join the strands at the bottom of the bread. It's as easy as that!

Serving Your Bread

Not only does the shape of your bread matter, but the way you present your bread to your guests also influences how your bread looks and tastes. Practice the following to ensure your bread is being showcased rather than reduced to just another food at the table. These tips aren't vital to the well-being of your bread, but they do make bread eating ten times more enjoyable.

Always use a serrated knife to cut your bread. Other knives will cause you to crush your bread. You should also let your bread cool a bit for the same reason. Warm bread easily gets squished. If it does squish, it will taste just as good, but it won't look like what you want or expect, and it will seem less impressive. Further, cutting slices too thin can also make your bread crumbly and ugly to serve, so aim or slightly thicker slices.

Serve your bread with butter. Fresh bread is excellent on its own, but it can be elevated with butter. If you'd like, you can even try taking your butter to the next level by infusing it with herbs or another seasoning. For Italian bread, you can stick to olive oil with a dipping bowl.

Fruit and cheese are excellent companions to bread. By serving these foods with bread, you're accentuating the flavors that you most want to accentuate. The more flavorful the bread, the more flavorful the cheese and fruit should be. You can do more research into cheese and bread pairings, but one example is that muenster cheese and red grapes can pair well with a loaf of country bread.

Ensure you are serving fresh bread. Plan so that for your dinner party or event, you can ensure that your bread was made that day. Bread will keep for a while, but it tastes best shortly after you've made it. Your guests will be delighted by a bread that is being pulled from the oven, and you'll be delighted by it too!

Let your fresh bread look and taste as wonderful as it can because it's a shame not to emphasize your hard work and talent as much as you can. Don't be afraid to show off. Making bread is an amazing feat, so you should be proud and want to display your beautiful creation properly before it is devoured.

Preserving Your Bread

While bread loaves are ideally served right away, some bread is meant to last for a whole week, or you have leftovers from the party (though, often, homemade bread goes fast in the circles I run in!). You'll need to find ways to preserve your bread as best as you can to keep it as fresh as it can be for as long as possible. There's nothing more disappointing than making a nice, big loaf and having it go stale before you've eaten it all.

Whatever you do, don't put already cooked loaves in the fridge. Bread dough can be stored in the fridge, but your fresh loaves will suffer in the fridge. Some experts say that bread that's placed in the fridge becomes stale six times faster than the bread you leave on your counter. Refrigeration is appropriate for store bread because of all the preservatives in store bread, but it is not appropriate for bread you make yourself (or bread you get from a bakery).

Keep in mind that different bread types will react differently. Breads that are lean and without much fat may stale faster. Thus, baguettes are ideally eaten as quickly as possible whereas brioche, which has more fat, can last longer. If your bread does go stale, you can make something with it. Cube it up and try making homemade croutons or make some stuffing out of it.

One way to preserve your bread is to freeze it, which will help lock in the flavors. You'll be able to delay the staling process for much longer, and by reheating it, you can help get some of the texture back into the bread. If you choose this route, be sure to put the bread in a freezer-safe container. Frozen bread will stay good for around two or three months. If you want to toast your frozen bread, you should slice it before you freeze it. Alternatively, if you don't plan to use the loaf in one sitting, cut it up into slices or chunks.

A breadbox is a good place to keep bread that you plan on using soon. It will keep the moisture levels food so that the bread won't get stale as quickly. Ceramic bread boxes are often what experts suggest, but you can also use enamelware or bamboo breadboxes that will do a good job as well. When you use a breadbox, do not bag your bread before placing it in the box.

If you don't have a breadbox and don't want to go through the fuss of freezing your bread, you can also wrap your bread in either foil or plastic. I have saved up old bread bags from the grocery store (sometimes even I have to grab a loaf from the supermarket) that I can put bread into in a pinch. Sealable plastic bags or foil also work. Be warned that these methods aren't ideal for storing bread, and the crust will lose some of its crunchiness, and the bread will be less moist as it starts to go stale. For bread that you plan on toasting, this option will work well because when toasted, the crust gets crunchy again.

Find the method that works best for you when it comes to bread preservation, but do your best to store it properly so that you can enjoy it as long as possible and as long as there's any bread left. Perfectly delicious bread should never go to waste, especially when you put so much work into it. With some attention and care, you can enjoy fresh bread throughout your week without having to worry too much about it going stale.

CONCLUSION

Thank you for making it through to the end of *Bread Baking*. I hope that it was enlightening and provided you with all of the tools you need to achieve your breadmaking goals. While I could write a dozen books on breadmaking and even after all that still have a plethora of information to give, this book should have given you the essential information on the topic.

The next step is to start making bread. Reading about bread making gives you the information that you need to get started, but breadmaking takes practice. You need to take this chance to get your hands dirty and take the chance on breadmaking. You might make some mistakes along the way, but that's a normal part of learning, so don't get discouraged if your first few loaves don't look as pretty as you want them to or if you mistakenly bake them too long. Even experienced bakers mess up loaves of bread once in a while, so it's okay to experiment and see what makes the best bread in your unique kitchen environment.

Feel free to try new recipes not included in this book and even make up your own because doing so is part of the joy of breadmaking. The more you practice, the more liberty you'll have to customize your creations.

Finally, if you found this book useful in any way, a review on Amazon is always appreciated! Enjoy your freshly baked loaves of bread and cherish your favorite recipes in this book!

www.ingramcontent.com/pod-product-compliance
Lightning Source LLC
Chambersburg PA
CBHW071814080526
44589CB00012B/785